BY THE EDITORS OF CONSUMER GUIDE®

CHINESE
COOKING CLASS
COOKBOOK

BEEKMAN HOUSE
NEW YORK

CONTENTS

Introduction 3

Appetizers 6
Stuffed Mushrooms • Green Onion Curls • Barbecued Pork • Gow Gees • Chicken and Banana Squares • Ham and Chicken Rolls • Dim Sims • Hors d'Oeuvre Rolls • Pork and Lettuce Rolls • Spring Rolls • Fried Wontons

Soups 18
Mongolian Hot Pot • Crab Combination Soup • Long Soup • Chicken and Corn Soup • Szechuan Soup

Meats 24
Satay Beef • Beef with Noodles • Beef with Black Bean Sauce • Beef with Cashews • Sherried Beef and Spinach • Steamed Pork Buns • Ginger Beef • Tenderloin Chinese Style • Beef with Peppers • Beef with Celery • Sweet and Sour Pork • Spiced Pork • Curried Beef • Beef Chow Mein

Poultry 40
Lemon Chicken • Sesame Chicken Salad • How to Chop Chicken Chinese Style • Honey Chili Chicken • Chicken with Lychees • Chicken with Water Chestnuts • Marinated Chicken Wings • Spiced Chicken • Chicken with Mangoes • Almond Chicken • Ginger Green Onion Chicken • Beggar's Chicken • Hoi Sin Chicken • Chicken Chow Mein • Combination Chop Suey • Honeyed Chicken and Pineapple • Braised Duck • Duck with Pineapple

Fish 60
Barbecued Shrimp • Seafood Combination • Scallops with Vegetables • Crab-Stuffed Shrimp • Shrimp Toast • Ginger Chili Fish • Crispy Fish with Lemon Sauce • Crab Claws • Shrimp Omelets • Butterfly Shrimp • Crab in Ginger Sauce • Braised Shrimp with Vegetables

Vegetables 74
Chinese Vegetables • Bean Curd with Oyster Sauce • Chinese Mixed Pickles

Rice and Noodles 78
Fried Rice • Vermicelli • Noodle Baskets • Fried Noodles • Steamed Rice

Desserts 84
Watermelon in Ginger Wine • Almond Crème • Banana Fritters • Lychees and Mandarin Ice • Melon with Champagne • Toffee Apples • Strawberry Sorbet • Chocolate Ginger Lychees • Custard Tarts • Sesame Peanut Candy • China Tea

Index 96

Library of Congress Catalog Card Number: 80-84040

ISBN: 0-517-322455

This edition published by:
Beekman House
A Division of Crown Publishers, Inc.
One Park Avenue
New York, N.Y. 10016
By arrangement with Publications International, Ltd.

Manufactured in the United States of America
2 3 4 5 6 7 8 9 10

INTRODUCTION

The Chinese are agricultural people, and their diets reflect that fact. Rice and vegetables predominate; soybeans are relied upon as a main source of protein. Meat, poultry and fish are not as important in Chinese cuisine as they are in many other cultures.

The Chinese are extremely creative in their cooking; it is estimated that there are over eighty thousand different dishes in Chinese cuisine. They are also artistic in the presentation of their food, believing that food should appeal to more than just the sense of taste. In addition to having good flavor, a dish should be fragrant, colorful and attractive. In a single meal, the various foods should have contrasting textures, and the flavors should maintain a balance between strong and subtle, spicy and bland.

China is a large country, covering over three million square miles in area. The various regions differ widely in climate, terrain and natural resources. These differences determine what kinds of foods are available in a particular region and, as a result, influence the cooking style in that region.

Four regional styles or schools of cooking exist in China: northern (including Peking, Shantung and Honan), coastal (Fukien and Shanghai), inland (Szechuan and Yunnan) and southern (Canton).

In the relatively cold northern region, wheat—not rice—is the staple food. Noodle dishes, steamed breads and dumplings are typical fare. Most of the dishes are light and delicate. Garlic and green onions are frequent flavorings, and spices, when used, are mild.

The coastal region has produced an abundance of fish and seafood recipes, along with many soups, including delicious, clear, light ones. Dishes from this region are usually well-seasoned with soy sauce. In fact, some of the most popular recipes call for meat, poultry or fish to be stewed in liquid that is liberally flavored with soy sauce. This is often referred to as "red cooking."

In the hot, almost tropical inland region, strongly seasoned, spicy foods are preferred. A widely used seasoning is Szechuan pepper, a piquant seasoning much more potent than the pepper commonly used in the United States. Deep-fried foods are popular in this region, too.

Most of the Chinese foods familiar to Americans come from the southern region surrounding Canton. Dishes characteristic of the Cantonese style are light, mildly seasoned and less greasy than those of the other three regions. Soy sauce, fresh ginger root, sherry and chicken stock are the most often used seasonings. The people in this region prefer to taste the natural flavors of the main ingredients of a recipe, rather than add extra spices. Many Cantonese dishes are prepared using the quick-cooking technique of stir-frying.

TECHNIQUES FOR CHINESE COOKING

Preparing tasty and attractive Chinese dishes can be a rewarding experience that is easy to accomplish. There are just a few rules to keep in mind for successfully cooking most recipes:

- Preparation and cooking are two separate procedures.
- All ingredients should be prepared *before* any cooking is begun.
- Exact timing is crucial because many of the foods are cooked over intense heat in a matter of minutes.

The Chinese have perfected a variety of cooking techniques, including stir-frying, deep-frying, braising, stewing, steaming, roasting, barbecuing and preserving. Except for stir-frying, all of these techniques are probably familiar to you. To stir-fry correctly, an understanding of its basic principles is necessary.

Stir-frying is a rapid-cooking method invented by the Chinese in ages past when cooking fuel was scarce. It is still the most frequently used of all Chinese cooking techniques. Stir-frying is the brisk cooking of small pieces of ingredients in hot oil over intense heat for a short time, usually just a few minutes. During cooking, the ingredients must be kept in constant motion by stirring or tossing vigorously. Once cooking is completed, the food should be removed immediately from the heat.

When stir-frying, all of the ingredients must be well organized and prepared *before cooking is started*. They should be measured or weighed, cleaned, chopped, sliced, combined or the like. The stir-frying is accomplished so quickly that there is usually not time to complete any preparation steps once cooking is begun.

Meat, poultry, fish and vegetables should be cut into pieces of uniform size for even cooking. Otherwise, one ingredient may be overcooked, while others remain undercooked.

The intensity of the heat used for stir-frying is important. In most cases, easily controlled high heat is needed. For this reason, a gas range with its ability for instant heat control is generally more efficient for stir-frying than is an electric range.

The type of oil used in stir-frying is also crucial. A vegetable oil that can be heated to a high temperature without smoking is essential. Peanut oil, corn oil, cottonseed oil and soybean oil all work well. Other kinds of fats, such as olive oil, sesame oil, butter, or lard, cannot be used because they have low burning points.

Success in stir-frying depends upon knowing what you are doing and why. Understanding the composition and textures of the ingredients you are using is essential, as is knowing how long each will take to cook—especially in relationship to the others.

Due to the variables that may be involved in stir-frying, such as kinds of food, type of heat available and the kind of cooking vessel used, cooking times listed in the recipes in this book should be used only as guidelines—not as absolutes. Most of the recipes, for example, were tested on a gas range. Cooking times needed when using a wok on an electric range or when using an electric wok may vary somewhat.

UTENSILS FOR CHINESE COOKING

A reasonably equipped kitchen usually contains more than enough utensils to adequately handle Chinese cooking. However, one item you may not have, but may wish to consider purchasing, is a wok, especially if you plan to make stir-fried dishes frequently. Invented many centuries ago, the wok is an all-purpose cooking pan used in virtually every Chinese household for almost every kind of cooking.

Traditionally, a wok was made from thin, tempered iron, and had a rounded bottom for fast, even conduction of heat. Some woks are, of course, still made that way. However, modern technology has brought some changes in the wok. In addition to iron, woks are now manufactured in aluminum, stainless steel and carbon steel. Woks with flat bottoms are made for use on electric ranges and on smooth-top cooking surfaces. There are electric woks with nonstick finishes and automatic thermostatic controls. On some woks, the customary thin metal handles positioned on two sides have been replaced with a single, long wooden handle. This version eliminates the necessity of keeping pot holders handy at all times to pick up or steady the wok. Deciding upon what kind of wok to purchase is a matter of personal preference. All of them are functional.

Woks range in size from 12 to 24 inches (30 to 60 cm) in diameter. The 14-inch (35 cm) size is a good choice for use as an all-purpose utensil. That size is adequate to handle most stir-frying and other cooking chores without interfering with the use of other burners on the range top.

Before a new iron or carbon steel wok is used, it should be washed and seasoned. Wash it thoroughly in hot, soapy water (the first time only) and use a scouring pad, if necessary, to remove any protective coating. Rinse the wok with water and dry it completely. Rub 1 tablespoon (15 mL) of vegetable oil completely over the interior of the wok. Place it over low heat until it is hot throughout (3 to 5 minutes); remove wok from heat and cool.

After each use, the wok should be soaked in hot water and cleaned with a bamboo brush or sponge. Do not clean the wok with soap or soap-treated scouring pads. Rinse the wok with water, dry it and place it over low heat until all water evaporates. Then rub 1 teaspoon (5 mL) of vegetable oil over the inside of the wok to keep it from rusting.

Another very useful utensil for Chinese cooking is a cleaver. It is not essential, but it is handy for slicing, chopping and mincing ingredients and is especially helpful for chopping whole chickens and ducks into Chinese-style serving pieces.

INGREDIENTS IN CHINESE CUISINE

When preparing Chinese foods, you will come across many ingredients that are familiar. You will also en-counter some that may be unfamiliar, such as hoi sin sauce, oyster sauce or five-spice powder. Some of the items—seasonings in particular—may be available only in Chinese food markets. Before you search for an out-of-the-way specialty store, however, check your local supermarket. Many supermarkets in cities and towns of all sizes are now stocking good inventories of Chinese ingredients. In addition to canned, bottled and packaged products, many even carry fresh items, such as Chinese cabbage, bean sprouts, wonton and egg-roll wrappers, bean curd and Chinese-style egg noodles. A check of the frozen-food cases probably will yield additional Chinese items.

As with any other kind of cooking, choose the freshest ingredients you can find, especially when purchasing vegetables, meat, poultry or fish. The Chinese are so conscientious about cooking with the freshest foods possible that they plan their menus around the foods they find in the market—rather than planning the marketing around the menu.

The glossary that follows describes many of the Chinese foods that are used in the recipes in this book.

GLOSSARY OF CHINESE INGREDIENTS

Bamboo shoots: tender, ivory-colored shoots of tropical bamboo plants, used separately as a vegetable and to add crispness and a slight sweetness to foods. They are available in cans—whole or sliced—and may be rinsed with water before using.

Barbecue sauce, Chinese: see satay sauce.

Bean curd (also called tofu): pureed soybeans pressed to form a white custard-like cake, used as a vegetable and as an excellent source of protein. Beans curd can be used in all kinds of recipes; although its own flavor is bland, its porosity enables it to absorb the flavors of other foods. Bean curd is available fresh or in cans. If fresh, it should be covered with water and stored in the refrigerator.

Bean sprouts: small, white shoots of the pea-like mung bean plant, used separately as a vegetable and included in a wide variety of dishes. They are available fresh or in cans. Canned sprouts should be rinsed before use to eliminate a metallic taste. Fresh or opened unused canned sprouts should be covered with water and stored in the refrigerator.

Bean threads (also called transparent or cellophane noodles): dry, hard, white, fine noodles made from powdered mung beans. They have little flavor of their own, but do readily absorb the flavors of other foods. Bean threads can be used in numerous steamed, simmered, deep-fried or stir-fried dishes. They are available in packets or small bundles.

Black beans, fermented: strongly flavored, preserved, small black soybeans. They are quite salty and are often used as a seasoning in combination with garlic. Fermented black beans are available in cans, bottles or plastic bags; they should be rinsed or soaked before using.

Cabbage, Chinese (also called bok-choy): a tender, delicate vegetable with white stalks and green, crinkled leaves. It requires very little cooking and is frequently included in soups and stir-fried dishes. Chinese cabbage is available fresh by the bunch.

Chili sauce, Chinese: a bright red, hot-flavored sauce made from crushed fresh chili peppers and salt. It is available in cans or bottles and should be used sparingly.

Egg noodles, Chinese: thin pasta usually made of flour, egg, water and salt. The noodles can be purchased fresh, frozen or dehydrated. They can be boiled, braised, stir-fried or deep-fried; the time and method of cooking vary with the type of noodle. Check the package for specific instructions.

Egg roll wrappers: commercially prepared dough made of flour and water, rolled very thinly, and cut into 7- or 8-inch (18 or 20 cm) squares. The wrappers are available fresh or frozen.

Five-spice powder: cocoa-colored, ready-mixed blend of five ground spices (usually anise seed, fennel, clove, cinnamon and ginger or pepper). It has a slightly sweet, pungent flavor and should be used sparingly.

Ginger root: a knobby, gnarled root, having a brown skin and whitish or light green interior. It has a fresh, pungent flavor and is used as a basic seasoning in many Chinese recipes. Ginger root is available fresh or in cans. It will keep for weeks in the refrigerator if wrapped in plastic or for months if kept in salted water or dry sherry. There really is no adequate substitute for the unique flavor of ginger root—not even ground ginger.

Hoi sin sauce: a thick, dark brown sauce made of soybeans, flour, sugar, spices, garlic, chili and salt. It has a sweet, spicy flavor and is called for in numerous Chinese recipes.

Lychee (also called lichee or litchi): a small, juicy, oval-shaped fruit with a bright red skin, white pulp and a large pit. Lychees have a delicate, sweet flavor. They are used in main dishes in combination with other foods or are served separately as a dessert or snack. Lychees are available in cans—whole, pitted and packed in syrup.

MSG (monosodium glutamate): a white, crystalline extract of dried, fermented wheat or soybean protein. It is frequently used as a seasoning, although it has almost no flavor of its own. It is thought that MSG heightens the flavors of foods with which it is combined. Its value is controversial and, for some people, MSG may have unpleasant side effects.

Mushrooms, dried: dehydrated black or brown mushrooms from the Orient, having caps from 1 to 3 inches (2.5 to 7.5 cm) in diameter. They have a strong, distinctive flavor and are included in many different kinds of recipes. Chinese dried mushrooms must be soaked in water before use; they are usually thinly sliced prior to combining them with other foods. The mushrooms are available in cellophane packages.

Oyster sauce: a thick, brown, concentrated sauce made of ground oysters, soy sauce and brine. It imparts very little fish flavor and is used as a seasoning to intensify other flavors. Oyster sauce is included in a variety of recipes, especially in stir-fried Cantonese-style dishes.

Parsley, Chinese (also called cilantro or fresh coriander): a strongly flavored, green herb with flat, broad leaves. It is commonly used fresh as a seasoning or garnish.

Peanut oil: a golden-colored oil pressed from peanuts, which has a light and slightly nutty flavor. This oil has a high smoking point which makes it ideal for stir-fried dishes. It is available in bottles or cans.

Plum sauce: a thick, piquant, chutney-like sauce frequently served with duck or pork dishes. It is available in cans or bottles.

Satay (Saté) sauce (also called Chinese barbecue sauce): a dark brown, hot, spicy sauce composed of soy sauce, ground shrimp, chili peppers, sugar, garlic, oil and spices. It is available in cans or jars.

Sesame oil: an amber-colored oil pressed from toasted sesame seeds. It has a strong, nut-like flavor and is best used sparingly. Sesame oil is generally employed only as a flavoring, not as a cooking medium, because it has a low smoking point. It is available in bottles.

Snow peas (also called Chinese peas or pea pods): flat, green pods that are picked before the peas have matured. They add crispness, color and flavor to foods, require very little cooking and are frequently used in stir-fried dishes. Snow peas are available fresh or frozen.

Soy sauce: a pungent, brown, salty liquid made of fermented soybeans, wheat, yeast, salt and, sometimes, sugar. It is an essential ingredient in Chinese cooking as a seasoning, flavor enhancer for other foods and a coloring. There are several types of Chinese soy sauces (light, dark, heavy), as well as Japanese-style soy sauce. The Japanese sauce fits between the Chinese light and dark varieties; it is the kind most commonly available in the United States and has been used in testing the recipes in this book. All types of soy sauce are available in bottles or large cans.

Szechuan pepper: a reddish-brown pepper having a strong, pungent aroma and a flavor with a time-delayed action—its numbing effect may not be noticed immediately. This pepper comes from the inland Szechuan province and is the main reason the food from that region tends to be so hot. This pepper should be used sparingly. It is usually sold whole or crushed—not ground—in small packages.

Water chestnut: a walnut-sized bulb from an aquatic plant. The bulb has a tough, brown skin and a crisp, white interior. Water chestnuts are served separately as a vegetable and are used to add crisp texture and a delicate, sweet flavor to other foods. They are available whole, peeled fresh or whole or sliced in cans.

Wonton wrappers: commercially prepared dough that is rolled thinly and cut into 3- to 4-inch (8 to 10 cm) squares. The wrappers are available fresh or frozen.

APPETIZERS

Stuffed Mushrooms

MUSHROOMS
24 fresh medium
   mushrooms (about
   1 pound or 450 g)
6 ounces (170 g) uncooked,
   boneless lean pork
¼ cup (60 mL) drained
   whole water chestnuts
   (¼ of 8 ounce or 225 g
   can)
3 green onions
½ small red or green
   pepper, seeded
1 small stalk celery
1 teaspoon (5 mL)
   cornstarch
1 teaspoon (5 mL) grated,
   pared fresh ginger root
2 teaspoons (10 mL) dry
   sherry
1 teaspoon (5 mL) soy
   sauce
½ teaspoon (2 mL) hoi
   sin sauce
1 egg white
3 cups (750 mL) vegetable
   oil
½ cup (125 mL) all-purpose
   flour

BATTER
½ cup (125 mL)
   cornstarch
½ cup (125 mL) all-purpose
   flour
1½ teaspoons (7 mL)
   baking powder
¾ teaspoon (4 mL) salt
⅓ cup (80 mL) milk
⅓ cup (80 mL) water

For Mushrooms
1. Clean mushrooms by wiping with a damp cloth. Remove stems, chop stems finely and transfer to large bowl.

2. Finely chop pork, water chestnuts, onions, pepper and celery with sharp knife or in food processor. Add to chopped mushroom stems. Add cornstarch, ginger, sherry, soy and hoi sin sauces and egg white. Mix well.

3. Spoon pork mixture into cavities of mushroom caps, mounding mixture in center.

4. Heat oil in wok over high heat until it reaches 375°F (190°C).

5. Prepare batter. Carefully dip mushrooms in flour, then in batter, coating completely. Fry 6 or 8 mushrooms at a time in hot oil until golden, about 5 minutes. Drain on absorbent paper.

For Batter
6. Combine cornstarch, flour, baking powder and salt in bowl. Blend in milk and water.

Makes 2 dozen

Green Onion Curls

Green onion curls are used frequently throughout this book as a garnish. Here are the instructions for preparing them.

6 to 8 fresh medium green
   onions
Cold water
10 to 12 ice cubes

1. Trim bulbs from onions at point where stems begin to turn green. Trim remaining stems to a length of about 4 inches (10 cm), cutting off tops if necessary. Reserve bulbs and remaining tops for another use.

2. Using sharp scissors, cut each section of the green stems lengthwise into very thin strips down to the beginning of the stem. Cut about 6 to 8 strips in each stem section.

3. Fill a medium or large bowl about half full of cold water. Place green onions in water. Add ice cubes. Refrigerate until onions curl, about 1 hour.

4. Drain onion curls. Use as garnish.

Makes 6 to 8 curls

Barbecued Pork

2 whole pork tenderloins
   (about 12 ounces or
   340 g each)
¼ cup (60 mL) soy sauce
2 tablespoons (30 mL) dry
   red wine
1 tablespoon (15 mL)
   brown sugar
1 tablespoon (15 mL) honey
2 teaspoons (10 mL) red
   food coloring, if desired
½ teaspoon (2 mL) ground
   cinnamon
1 clove garlic, crushed
1 green onion, cut in half
Green Onion Curls
   (see recipe above), if
   desired

4. Bake in preheated 350°F (180°C) oven until done, about 45 minutes. Turn and baste frequently during baking.

1. Remove and discard fat from meat.

2. Combine soy sauce, wine, sugar, honey, food coloring, cinnamon, garlic and onion in large bowl. Add pork, turning tenderloins to coat completely. Cover and let stand at room temperature 1 hour or refrigerate overnight, turning occasionally.

3. Drain pork, reserving marinade. Place pork on wire rack over a baking pan.

5. Remove pork from oven. Cool. Cut into diagonal slices. Garnish with Green Onion Curls.

Makes about 8 appetizer servings

Gow Gees

SWEET AND SOUR SAUCE
1 cup (250 mL) water
½ cup (125 mL) white vinegar
½ cup (125 mL) sugar
¼ cup (60 mL) tomato paste
4 teaspoons (20 mL) cornstarch

GOW GEES
1 ounce (30 g) dried mushrooms
Boiling water
48 wonton wrappers (about 1 pound or 450 g)
2 ounces (60 g) shrimp
4 ounces (115 g) uncooked boneless lean pork
3 green onions
2 teaspoons (10 mL) soy sauce
½ teaspoon (2 mL) grated pared fresh ginger root
1 small clove garlic, crushed
3 cups (750 mL) vegetable oil

For Sauce

1. Combine water, vinegar, sugar, tomato paste and cornstarch in small saucepan. Cook over medium heat, stirring constantly, until sauce boils. Boil and stir 1 minute. Keep sauce warm.

For Gow Gees

2. Place mushrooms in bowl and cover with boiling

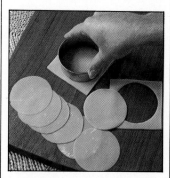

water. Let stand 30 minutes. Drain and squeeze out excess water.

3. Cut wonton wrappers into circles using 3-inch (8 cm) biscuit or cookie cutter. Cover wrappers with plastic wrap to avoid excessive drying.

4. Remove shells and back veins from shrimp. Finely chop shrimp, pork, onions and mushrooms with cleaver, sharp knife or food processor. Transfer chopped foods to large

bowl. Add soy sauce, ginger and garlic. Mix well.

5. Place level teaspoon (5 mL) pork mixture onto center of each wonton circle. Brush edges with water. Fold circles in half over filling, pressing edges firmly together to seal.

6. Heat vegetable oil in wok over high heat until it reaches 375°F (190°C). Fry 8 to 10 gow gees at a time in hot oil until golden, 2 to 3 minutes. Drain on absorbent paper. Serve with Sweet and Sour Sauce.
Makes 4 dozen

Chicken and Banana Squares

2 whole chicken breasts, cooked
6 slices white sandwich bread
2 firm medium bananas
4 eggs
½ cup (125 mL) milk
½ cup (125 mL) all-purpose flour
4 cups (1 L) soft bread crumbs (from 8 to 10 bread slices)
3 cups (750 mL) vegetable oil

1. Cut cooked chicken breasts in half. Carefully remove skin and bones from chicken. Cut each of the chicken pieces in half lengthwise, yielding 8 pieces. Cut each of those pieces into thirds, yielding 24 pieces total.

2. Remove and discard crusts from bread. Cut each slice into quarters.

3. Peel bananas. Cut each banana lengthwise into quarters. Cut each quarter into thirds, yielding 12 pieces per banana.

4. Beat eggs and milk in bowl with fork until blended. Brush egg mixture over one side of each of the 24 bread pieces. Place one

piece of chicken and one piece of banana on eggglazed side of each bread piece.

5. Place flour in one bowl and bread crumbs in another bowl. Coat each chicken and banana square lightly with flour, then dip in egg mixture and coat with bread crumbs. Dip again in egg mixture and coat with crumbs.

6. Heat oil in wok over high heat until it reaches 375°F (190°C). Fry 4 or 6 squares at a time in hot oil until golden, 2 to 3 minutes. Drain on absorbent paper.
Makes 2 dozen

Ham and Chicken Rolls

2 whole chicken breasts
½ teaspoon (2 mL) salt
¼ teaspoon (1 mL) pepper
¼ teaspoon (1 mL) five-
spice powder
⅛ teaspoon (0.5 mL) garlic
powder
4 slices cooked ham (about
1 ounce or 30 g each)
1 egg, beaten
2 tablespoons (30 mL) milk
¼ cup (60 mL) all-purpose
flour
4 spring roll or egg roll
wrappers
3 cups (750 mL) vegetable
oil

1. Remove skin from chicken and discard. Cut breasts in half. Remove and discard bones. Pound chicken breasts until very thin using a mallet or rolling pin.

2. Combine salt, pepper, five-spice powder and garlic powder. Sprinkle about ¼ teaspoon (1 mL) of the mixture evenly over each flattened chicken piece.

3. Tightly roll up each ham slice and place on top of a chicken piece. Roll chicken around ham, tucking in ends.

4. Combine egg and milk in shallow dish. Coat each chicken piece lightly with flour, then dip into egg-milk mixture. Place each piece diagonally onto a spring roll wrapper. Roll up securely, folding in the ends. Brush the end corner with egg mixture and pinch to seal.

5. Heat oil in wok over high heat until it reaches 375°F (190°C). Fry 3 or 4 rolls at a time in the hot oil until golden and chicken is completely cooked, about 5 minutes. Drain on absorbent paper. Cool slightly. Cut into 1-inch (2.5 cm) diagonal slices to serve.

Makes 4 rolls

Dim Sims

8 ounces (225 g) uncooked
medium shrimp
1 pound (450 g) uncooked
boneless lean pork
¼ head small cabbage
(about 4 ounces or
115 g)
6 green onions
2 eggs, slightly beaten
3 tablespoons (45 mL)
cornstarch
4 teaspoons (20 mL) soy
sauce
1 tablespoon (15 mL)
sesame oil
2 teaspoons (10 mL) oyster
sauce
48 wonton wrappers (about
1 pound or 450 g)
3 cups (750 mL) vegetable
oil

1. Remove shells and back veins from shrimp. Finely chop shrimp, pork, cabbage and onions with cleaver, sharp knife or food processor. Transfer chopped foods to large bowl. Add eggs, cornstarch, soy sauce, sesame oil and oyster sauce. Mix well.

2. Place rounded teaspoon of mixture onto center of each wonton wrapper.

3. Gently press wrappers around filling, tucking edges together as shown but leaving tops open. (To avoid excessive drying, work with about 12 wrappers at a time.)

4. Heat vegetable oil in wok over high heat until it reaches 375°F (190°C). Fry 8

to 10 dim sims at a time in hot oil until golden, 2 to 3 minutes. Drain on absorbent paper.

Makes 4 dozen

Hors d'Oeuvre Rolls

½ cup (125 mL) Chinese fine egg noodles, broken into 1-inch (2.5 cm) pieces
8 ounces (225 g) cooked shelled and deveined shrimp
4 ounces (115 g) uncooked boneless lean pork
6 fresh medium mushrooms
6 green onions
1 hard-cooked egg
2 tablespoons (30 mL) butter or margarine
1½ tablespoons (22 mL) dry sherry
½ teaspoon (2 mL) salt
⅛ teaspoon (0.5 mL) pepper
2 sheets commercial puff pastry dough or 40 wonton wrappers
1 egg, beaten
3 cups (750 mL) vegetable oil
Sweet and Sour Sauce (see Index for page number), if desired

1. Cook noodles until tender according to package directions. Drain and chop finely.

2. Finely chop shrimp, pork, mushrooms, onions and hard-cooked egg with cleaver, sharp knife or food processor.

3. Heat butter in skillet or wok over medium-high heat. Stir-fry pork in the butter until brown, about 5 minutes. Add mushrooms and onions. Stir-fry 2

minutes. Remove from heat and add shrimp, hard-cooked egg, noodles, sherry, salt and pepper. Mix well.

4. If using puff pastry, roll and trim each sheet into a

15 x 12-inch (38 x 30 cm) rectangle. Cut into 20 (3 inch or 8 cm) squares.

5. Place a tablespoon (15 mL) of pork mixture across center of each pastry square or wonton wrapper. Brush

edges lightly with beaten egg. Roll up wrapper tightly around filling. Pinch ends slightly to seal.

6. Heat oil in wok over high heat until it reaches 375°F (190°C). Fry 6 or 8 rolls at a time in the hot oil until golden, 3 to 5 minutes. Drain on absorbent paper. Serve with Sweet and Sour Sauce.

Makes 40 rolls

Pork and Lettuce Rolls

1 ounce (30 g) dried mushrooms
Boiling water
8 ounces (225 g) uncooked boneless lean pork
½ cup (125 mL) drained sliced bamboo shoots (½ of 8 ounce or 225 g can)
½ cup (125 mL) drained whole water chestnuts (½ of 8 ounce or 225 g can)
6 green onions
1 can (6½ ounces or 185 g) crabmeat
1 tablespoon (15 mL) vegetable oil
2 tablespoons (30 mL) dry sherry
1 tablespoon (15 mL) soy sauce
2 teaspoons (10 mL) oyster sauce
2 teaspoons (10 mL) sesame oil
9 Iceberg lettuce leaves

1. Place mushrooms in bowl and cover with boiling water. Let stand 30 minutes. Drain. Remove and discard stems.

2. Finely chop pork, mushroom caps, bamboo shoots, water chestnuts and onions. Drain and flake crabmeat.

3. Heat vegetable oil in wok over high heat. Stir-fry pork in the oil until golden, 6 to 8 minutes. Add mushrooms, bamboo shoots, water chestnuts, onions and crabmeat. Stir-fry 1 minute.

4. Combine sherry, soy sauce, oyster sauce and sesame oil. Stir into pork mixture. Remove from heat.

5. Place about ⅓ cup (80 mL) pork mixture onto center of each lettuce leaf.

6. Fold ends and sides of lettuce leaves over filling and roll up. Arrange on serving plate. If desired, pork and lettuce leaves may be served separately and rolled at the table.

Makes 9 rolls

Spring Rolls

1 pound (450 g) uncooked medium shrimp
1 pound (450 g) uncooked boneless lean pork
4 ounces (115 g) fresh mushrooms, cleaned
8 green onions
1 red pepper, seeded
8 ounces (225 g) Chinese cabbage (about ½ of a head)
1 can (8 ounces or 225 g) water chestnuts, drained
3 tablespoons (45 mL) dry sherry
1½ tablespoons (22 mL) soy sauce
2 teaspoons (10 mL) grated pared fresh ginger root
1 teaspoon (5 mL) sugar
½ teaspoon (2 mL) salt
¼ cup (60 mL) water
1½ tablespoons (22 mL) cornstarch
24 spring roll or egg roll wrappers
3 cups (750 mL) vegetable oil

1. Remove shells and back veins from shrimp. Remove and discard fat from pork. Finely chop shrimp, pork, mushrooms, onions, pepper, cabbage and water chestnuts using cleaver, sharp knife or food processor.

2. Transfer all chopped ingredients to large mixing bowl. Add sherry, soy sauce, ginger, sugar and salt. Mix well.

3. Mix water and cornstarch in small bowl until blended.

4. Place ¼ cup (60 mL) of the pork mixture evenly across a corner of each wrapper. Brush cornstarch mixture evenly over all edges of wrappers. Carefully roll wrappers around filling, folding in the corners.

5. Heat oil in wok over high heat until it reaches 375°F (190°C). Fry 3 or 4 rolls at a time in the hot oil until golden, 3 to 5 minutes. Drain on absorbent paper.
Makes 2 dozen

Fried Wontons

1 ounce (30 g) dried mushrooms
Boiling water
1 pound (450 g) uncooked boneless lean pork
4 ounces (115 g) fresh spinach
1½ tablespoons (22 mL) dry sherry
4 teaspoons (20 mL) soy sauce
¼ teaspoon (1 mL) pepper
48 wonton wrappers (about 1 pound or 450 g)
1 can (6 ounces or 170 g) pineapple juice
½ cup (125 mL) white vinegar
1 tablespoon (15 mL) catsup
½ cup (125 mL) sugar
¼ cup (60 mL) water
1½ tablespoons (22 mL) cornstarch
½ cup (125 mL) Chinese Mixed Pickles (see Index for page number)
3 cups (750 mL) vegetable oil

Reduce heat, cook and stir 3 minutes. Stir in Chinese Mixed Pickles. Keep warm.

6. Heat oil in wok over medium-high heat until it reaches 375°F (190°C). Fry 8 to 10 wontons at a time in hot oil until golden, 2 to 3 minutes. Drain on absor-

1. Place mushrooms in bowl and cover with boiling water. Let stand 30 minutes. Drain and squeeze out excess water.

2. Finely chop pork, spinach and mushrooms with cleaver, sharp knife or food processor. Transfer chopped foods to large bowl. Add sherry, 2 teaspoons (10 mL) of the soy sauce and the pepper. Mix well.

3. Spoon a rounded teaspoon of mixture onto center of each wonton wrapper. (To avoid excessive drying, work with about 12 wrappers at a time.)

4. Gather edges of wrapper around filling, pressing firmly at top to seal.

5. Combine pineapple juice, vinegar, catsup, sugar and remaining 2 teaspoons (10 mL) soy sauce in small saucepan. Bring to boil. Blend water and cornstarch. Stir into pineapple mixture.

bent paper. To serve, pour pineapple mixture over wontons.

Makes 4 dozen

Mongolian Hot Pot

Mongolian Hot Pot or Chinese Steamboat—this dish has several names, any of which translate into a meal that's delicious and fun. Traditionally it's cooked in an Oriental fire pot, which has a chamber under the food basin to hold hot charcoal. This unique pot is not essential to the success of this dish, though. A chafing dish, fondue pot, an electric wok or fry pan are just as functional but much less dramatic.

Mongolian Hot Pot is an easy way to entertain since each diner cooks his or her own meal at the table. The pot is placed in the center of the table and filled with simmering stock. Each diner chooses his own meal from a variety of prepared meat, fish and vegetable offerings then cooks it, piece by piece, in the stock. When all of the food has been cooked, the stock (which has since become a richly flavored soup) serves as the final course.

Small bowls of assorted Chinese-style accompaniments may be offered, including soy sauce, chili sauce, hoi sin sauce, barbecue sauce or lemon sauce. Freshly steamed rice and tea would appropriately round out the meal.

STOCK
10 cups (2.5 L) water
2 whole chicken breasts
1 medium yellow onion, sliced
2 stalks celery, cut into ½-inch (1.5 cm) slices
1 tablespoon (15 mL) instant chicken bouillon granules
2 tablespoons (30 mL) dry sherry

1 teaspoon (5 mL) sesame oil
1 piece (2x1 inches or 5x2.5 cm) fresh ginger root, cut into thin slices

HOT POT
1 whole beef tenderloin (about 12 ounces or 340 g)
1 whole pork tenderloin (about 12 ounces or 340 g)
8 ounces (225 g) chicken livers
2 whole chicken breasts
1 pound (450 g) fresh or thawed frozen fish fillets
1 pound (450 g) fresh medium shrimp
2 dozen fresh oysters in the shell, if desired
½ head small Chinese cabbage
8 ounces (225 g) fresh spinach
8 green onions
1 medium cucumber or zucchini
1 can (8 ounces or 225 g) sliced bamboo shoots
8 ounces (225 g) bean curd

For Stock
1. Combine all ingredients in 5-quart (5 L) Dutch oven. Cover and bring to boil. Reduce heat to low and simmer stock about 2 hours. Strain stock.

For Hot Pot
2. Remove and discard fat from beef and pork tenderloins. Wrap each tenderloin in plastic wrap and freeze 45 to 60 minutes. Cut meat across the grain into ⅛-inch (0.5 cm) slices. Rinse chicken livers, trim and cut into ½-inch (1.5 cm) slices. Remove skin and bones from chicken and discard. Cut chicken into 1-inch (2.5 cm) square pieces. Remove skin, if any, from fish. Cut fish into 1-inch (2.5 cm) pieces. Remove shells and back veins from shrimp. Remove oysters from shells and rinse with water. Arrange all meat, chicken and fish on serving plates. Cover with plastic wrap and refrigerate.

3. Rinse vegetables with water. Shred cabbage. Remove stems from spinach and cut spinach into ½-inch (1.5 cm) wide strips. Cut onions into 2-inch (5 cm) pieces. Cut cucumber into thin slices. Drain bamboo shoots. Cut bean curd into 2x¼-inch (5x0.5 cm) slices. Arrange all vegetables on serving plates.

4. To prepare fire pot: burn about 24 charcoal briquets in outdoor hibachi or barbecue grill until white-hot. Using long tongs, tightly pack the coals inside cooking chamber of fire pot. Place pot on a thick board to absorb the heat and protect tabletop.

5. Heat stock until boiling. Pour stock into top of fire pot or other cooking utensil. Uncover trays of meat and vegetables. Provide each diner with small strainers, slotted spoons or chop sticks to hold food. Cook food by placing in simmering stock until done. Remove from stock and drain slightly. Place on plates.
Makes 8 to 10 servings

Crab Combination Soup

1 ounce (30 g) dried
    mushrooms
Boiling water
6 ounces (170 g) fresh or
    thawed frozen crabmeat
4 ounces (115 g) fresh or
    thawed frozen sea
    scallops
½ cup (125 mL) drained
    whole or sliced bamboo
    shoots (½ of 8 ounce or
    225 g can)
8 green onions
1 teaspoon (5 mL)
    vegetable oil
1 egg, slightly beaten
6 cups (1.5 L) chicken broth
½ teaspoon (2 mL) grated
    pared fresh ginger root
3 tablespoons (45 mL)
    cornstarch
6 tablespoons (90 mL)
    water
1½ tablespoons (22 mL)
    dry sherry
4 teaspoons (20 mL) soy
    sauce
2 egg whites

1. Place mushrooms in bowl and cover with boiling water. Let stand 30 minutes. Drain. Remove and discard stems. Cut caps into thin slices.

2. Flake crabmeat. Rinse scallops with water, drain and cut into thin slices. Cut

bamboo shoots into thin strips. Chop green onions.

3. Heat oil in small omelet or crepe pan. Add egg and tilt pan so egg completely covers bottom. Cook over

medium-high heat until egg is set. Loosen edges and turn omelet over to cook other side. Remove from pan, roll up and cut into thin strips.

4. Pour broth into 3-quart (3 L) saucepan. Cook over high heat until broth boils. Stir in mushrooms, crabmeat, scallops, bamboo shoots, onions, sliced egg, ginger and pepper. Return soup to boil.

5. Combine cornstarch, 4 tablespoons (60 mL) of the water, the sherry and soy sauce. Stir mixture into soup. Return soup to boil.

6. Beat egg whites and remaining 2 tablespoons (30

mL) water. Drizzle egg whites slowly into soup while stirring soup vigorously.

Makes 6 servings

Long Soup

8 green onions
4 to 6 ounces (115 to 170 g)
    cabbage (¼ of small
    head)
8 ounces (225 g) uncooked
    boneless lean pork
1½ tablespoons (22 mL)
    vegetable oil
6 cups (1.5 L) chicken stock
    or broth
2 tablespoons (30 mL) soy
    sauce
½ teaspoon (2 mL) grated
    pared fresh ginger root
4 ounces (115 g) thin
    Chinese egg noodles

1. Cut onions into thin diagonal slices. Shred cabbage. Slice pork into thin strips.

2. Heat oil in wok over medium-high heat. Stir-fry until pork is no longer pink, about 5 minutes.

3. Add stock, soy sauce and ginger to pork mixture. Cook until mixture boils. Reduce heat and simmer 10 minutes.

4. Stir in noodles and onions. Cook just until noodles are tender, 1 to 4 minutes.

Makes about 4 servings

Chicken and Corn Soup

6¾ cups (1685 mL) water
2 pounds (900 g) chicken pieces*
6 whole peppercorns
1½ teaspoons (7 mL) salt
1 or 2 sprigs fresh parsley, if desired
1 medium yellow onion
1 piece (about 1-inch or 2.5 cm square) fresh ginger root
8 green onions
1 can (about 16 ounces or 450 g) cream-style corn
2 teaspoons (10 mL) instant chicken bouillon granules
1 teaspoon (5 mL) sesame oil
½ teaspoon (2 mL) grated pared fresh ginger root
⅛ teaspoon (0.5 mL) ground pepper
¼ cup (60 mL) cornstarch
2 egg whites
2 slices (about 1 ounce or 30 g each) cooked ham

*Note: Any kind of chicken pieces may be used including necks and backs. Enough meat should be on the chicken pieces to yield the 1 cup (250 mL) shredded cooked chicken that will be needed in the soup.

1. Combine 6 cups (1.5 L) of the water, the chicken pieces, whole peppercorns, 1 teaspoon (5 mL) of the salt and the parsley in 5-quart (5 L) Dutch oven. Cut yellow onion into thin slices. Pare the piece of ginger root and cut into thin slices. Add onion and ginger to chicken-water mixture. Cover pan and cook over medium heat until water boils. Reduce heat to low. Simmer 1½ hours. Remove any scum or fat from top of stock. Strain stock. Return stock to pan. Cut enough chicken meat off from bones and shred with cleaver or sharp knife to yield 1 cup (250 mL) chicken.

2. Finely chop 4 of the green onions. Add the chopped onions, corn, bouillon, sesame oil, the grated ginger, pepper and remaining ½ teaspoon (2 mL) salt to stock. Cook over medium heat until stock boils.

3. Blend cornstarch and ½ cup (125 mL) of the remaining water. Stir mixture into stock. Cook and stir until soup thickens.

4. Beat egg whites and the remaining ¼ cup (60 mL) water lightly with fork. Drizzle egg whites slowly into stock while stirring stock vigorously.

5. Cut ham into "matchstick" thin strips about 1½ inches (4 cm) long. Stir ham and chicken into stock.

6. Pour soup into bowls. Cut remaining green onions into thin slices. Sprinkle slices over soup.
Makes 6 to 8 servings

Szechuan Soup

1 ounce (30 g) dried mushrooms
Boiling water
6 ounces (170 g) uncooked boneless lean pork
4 ounces (115 g) cooked ham
1 small red pepper
8 green onions
½ cup (125 mL) water chestnuts
8 ounces (225 g) bean curd
2 quarts (2 L) chicken stock
½ cup (125 mL) dry white wine
4 teaspoons (20 mL) soy sauce
½ teaspoon (2 mL) Chinese chili sauce
2½ tablespoons (37 mL) cornstarch
5 tablespoons (75 mL) water
2 teaspoons (10 mL) vinegar
1 teaspoon (5 mL) sesame oil
1 egg
8 ounces (225 g) uncooked shrimp, shelled and deveined

1. Place mushrooms in bowl and cover with boiling water. Let stand 30 minutes. Drain. Remove and discard stems. Cut caps into thin slices.

2. Cut pork and ham into "match-stick" thin strips. Remove seeds from pepper

and cut pepper into thin strips. Chop onions finely. Cut water chestnuts into slices. Cut bean curd into ½-inch (1.5 cm) cubes.

3. Combine chicken stock, wine, soy sauce and chili sauce in 5-quart (5 L) Dutch oven. Cook over medium

heat until soup boils. Reduce heat and simmer uncovered 5 minutes.

4. Blend cornstarch and 4 tablespoons (60 mL) of the water. Slowly stir mixture into soup. Cook and stir until soup boils. Add mushrooms, pork, ham, pepper and water chestnuts. Simmer uncovered 5 minutes.

5. Stir vinegar and oil into soup. Beat egg and remaining 1 tablespoon (15 mL) water together with fork. Gradually drizzle egg into soup while stirring soup vigorously. Add onions, bean curd and shrimp. Cook until shrimp is done, 1 to 2 minutes.
Makes 6 to 8 servings

MEATS

Satay Beef

1 pound (450 g) beef
   tenderloin
5 tablespoons (75 mL)
   water
1 teaspoon (5 mL)
   cornstarch
3½ teaspoons (17 mL) soy
   sauce
1 to 2 teaspoons (5 to 10 mL)
   sesame oil
2 tablespoons (30 mL)
   vegetable oil
1 medium onion, coarsely
   chopped
1 clove garlic, crushed
1 tablespoon (15 mL) dry
   sherry
1 tablespoon (15 mL) satay
   sauce
1 teaspoon (5 mL) curry
   powder
½ teaspoon (2 mL) sugar
Green onions, if desired

1. Remove and discard fat
from meat. Cut meat across
the grain into thin slices.
Flatten each slice slightly by
pressing with fingers.

2. Combine 3 tablespoons
(45 mL) of the water, the
cornstarch, 1½ teaspoons
(7 mL) of the soy sauce and
the sesame oil in medium
bowl. Mix in meat. Let stand
20 minutes.

3. Heat vegetable oil in wok
over high heat. Add half of
the meat to wok, spreading
out slices so they do not
overlap. Cook slices on each
side just until light brown, 2

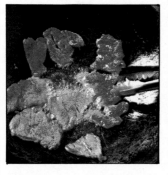

to 3 minutes. Remove meat
from wok. Repeat with re-
maining meat, then remove
it from wok.

4. Add onion and garlic to
wok. Stir-fry until onion is
soft, about 3 minutes.

5. Combine remaining 2
tablespoons (30 mL) water,
2 teaspoons (10 mL) soy
sauce, the sherry, satay
sauce, curry powder and
sugar. Add mixture to
onions. Cook and stir until
liquid boils. Mix in meat.
Garnish with thinly sliced
green onions.
Makes 4 servings

Beef with Noodles

8 ounces (225 g) Chinese fine egg noodles
½ cup (125 mL) water
3 teaspoons (15 mL) soy sauce
¼ teaspoon (1 mL) salt
2 teaspoons (10 mL) instant chicken bouillon granules
6 tablespoons (90 mL) vegetable oil
1 pound (450 g) beef rump steak
6 green onions
1 piece fresh ginger root (about 1-inch or 2.5 cm square)
2 cloves garlic

1. Cook noodles until tender according to package directions. Drain well. Place a clean towel over wire cooling racks. Spread noodles evenly over towel and dry about 3 hours.

2. Combine water, 2 teaspoons (10 mL) of the soy sauce, the salt and bouillon.

3. Heat 4 tablespoons (60 mL) of the oil in wok over high heat. Stir-fry noodles in the oil 3 minutes. Pour water mixture over noodles. Toss noodles until completely coated, about 2 minutes. Transfer noodles to serving plate. Keep warm.

4. Remove and discard fat from meat. Cut meat across the grain into thin slices about 2 inches (5 cm) long. Cut onions into thin diagonal slices. Pare ginger root and cut into thin slices. Crush or mince garlic.

5. Heat remaining 2 tablespoons (30 mL) oil in wok over high heat. Add beef, onions, ginger, garlic and remaining 1 teaspoon (5 mL) soy sauce. Stir-fry until beef is done, about 5 minutes. Spoon meat mixture over noodles.

Makes 4 servings

Beef with Black Bean Sauce

1½ pounds (675 g) beef rump steak
2½ tablespoons (37 mL) soy sauce
1½ tablespoons (22 mL) dry sherry
3 teaspoons (15 mL) cornstarch
1 egg white
⅔ cup (160 mL) water
1½ tablespoons (22 mL) fermented, salted black beans
¼ teaspoon (1 mL) sugar
4 tablespoons (60 mL) vegetable oil
4 green onions, cut into 1-inch (2.5 cm) pieces
1 red pepper, seeded and cut into thin slices
½ cup (125 mL) drained sliced bamboo shoots (½ of 8 ounce or 225 g can)
1 teaspoon (5 mL) curry powder

4. Add remaining 2 tablespoons (30 mL) oil to wok. Add meat and marinade. Stir-fry until meat is brown, about 5 minutes. Add vegetables and bean mixture to meat; mix well. Combine remaining ⅓ cup (80 mL)

1. Cut meat across the grain into thin slices 2 inches (5 cm) long. Combine soy sauce, sherry, 1 teaspoon (5 mL) of the cornstarch and the egg white in medium glass or plastic bowl; beat lightly with fork. Mix in meat. Let stand 30 minutes, stirring occasionally.

2. Combine ⅓ cup (80 mL) of the water and the beans in small bowl. Let stand 15 minutes. Drain beans, re-

serving 1 teaspoon (5 mL) of the water. Combine beans, the reserved water and the sugar on small plate. Mash well with fork.

3. Heat 2 tablespoons (30 mL) of the oil in wok over high heat. Add onions, pepper, bamboo shoots and curry powder. Stir-fry until vegetables are crisp-tender, 2 minutes. Remove mixture from wok.

water and 2 teaspoons (10 mL) cornstarch. Pour over meat-vegetable mixture. Cook and stir until liquid boils and thickens.

Makes 4 servings

Beef with Cashews

1 pound (450 g) beef rump
  steak
4 tablespoons (60 mL)
  vegetable oil
8 green onions
2 cloves garlic
1 piece fresh ginger root
  (about 1-inch or 2.5 cm
  square)
⅔ cup (160 mL) unsalted,
  roasted cashews (about 3
  ounces or 85 g)
½ cup (125 mL) water
4 teaspoons (20 mL)
  cornstarch
4 teaspoons (20 mL) soy
  sauce
1 teaspoon (5 mL) sesame
  oil
1 teaspoon (5 mL) oyster
  sauce
1 teaspoon (5 mL) Chinese
  chili sauce

1. Remove and discard fat from meat. Cut meat across the grain into thin slices about 2 inches (5 cm) long. Heat 2 tablespoons (30 mL) of the vegetable oil in wok over high heat. Stir-fry half of the meat in oil until brown, 3 to 5 minutes. Remove from wok. Cook remaining meat and remove from wok.

2. Cut green onions into 1-inch (2.5 cm) pieces. Crush garlic. Pare ginger and chop finely.

3. Heat remaining 2 tablespoons (30 mL) vegetable oil in wok over high heat. Add onions, garlic, ginger and cashews. Stir-fry 1 minute.

4. Mix meat into cashew-vegetable mixture. Combine all remaining ingredients and pour over meat mixture. Cook and stir until liquid boils and thickens.

Makes 4 servings

Sherried Beef and Spinach

1 pound (450 g) beef
  tenderloin
3 tablespoons (45 mL) dry
  sherry
1½ tablespoons (22 mL)
  soy sauce
1 teaspoon (5 mL) sugar
½ teaspoon (2 mL) sesame
  oil
1 pound (450 g) fresh
  spinach
1 piece fresh ginger root
  (2x1 inches or 5x2.5 cm)
3 tablespoons (45 mL)
  vegetable oil
2 tablespoons (30 mL)
  water
½ teaspoon (2 mL)
  cornstarch
1 teaspoon (5 mL) instant
  chicken bouillon
  granules

1. Remove and discard fat from meat. Cut meat across the grain into thin slices. Cut each slice in half. Flatten meat slightly by pressing with fingers.

2. Combine sherry, soy sauce, sugar and sesame oil in medium glass bowl. Mix in meat. Cover and refrigerate 2 hours, stirring occasionally.

3. Rinse spinach well under running water. Shake off excess water. Cut leaves into large pieces. If spinach has thick stems, remove them and cut into ½-inch (1.5 cm) diagonal slices. Pare ginger and cut into thin slices.

4. Heat 2 tablespoons (30 mL) of the vegetable oil in wok over high heat. Stir-fry ginger and spinach stems in oil 2 minutes. Remove from wok.

5. Add remaining 1 tablespoon (15 mL) vegetable oil to wok. Drain meat, reserving sherry mixture. Add half of the meat to wok, spreading out slices so they do not overlap. Cook slices on each side just until light brown, 2 to 3 minutes. Remove meat from wok. Repeat with remaining meat, and remove from wok.

6. Blend water, cornstarch and bouillon into sherry mixture. Add mixture to wok and cook until mixture boils, 1 to 2 minutes. Add spinach leaves, stems and ginger. Cook and stir until spinach is wilted, 3 minutes. Mix in meat. Cook and stir 1 minute longer.

Makes 4 servings

Steamed Pork Buns

2 tablespoons (30 mL) hoi sin sauce

1½ tablespoons (22 mL) oyster sauce

1½ tablespoons (22 mL) soy sauce

½ teaspoon (2 mL) sesame oil

8 ounces (225 g) Barbecued Pork (see Index for page number)

4 green onions

2 tablespoons (30 mL) vegetable oil

2 teaspoons (10 mL) grated pared fresh ginger root

1 clove garlic, crushed

1¼ cups (310 mL) water

1 tablespoon (15 mL) cornstarch

3 cups (750 mL) all-purpose flour

1 tablespoon (15 mL) baking powder

½ teaspoon (2 mL) salt

¼ cup (60 mL) vegetable shortening or lard

1 teaspoon (5 mL) white vinegar

Water

Note: These buns are cooked in bamboo steamers which are available in Chinese and specialty gourmet cookware stores. The round steamers can be purchased in various sizes separately or in sets of two or three tiers. For cooking, the covered steamer(s) is (are) placed over boiling water in a wok or large saucepan.

1. Combine hoi sin sauce, oyster sauce, soy sauce and sesame oil. Chop pork and onions finely.

2. Heat vegetable oil in wok or fry pan over high heat. Stir-fry ginger and garlic in the oil 1 minute. Stir in hoi sin mixture. Cook and stir 2 minutes. Combine ½ cup (125 mL) of the water and the cornstarch. Blend into hoi sin mixture. Cook and stir until liquid boils. Reduce heat to medium and simmer 2 minutes. Stir in pork and onions. Remove from heat. Cool completely.

3. Combine flour, baking powder and salt in large bowl. Cut or rub in shortening until mixture resembles bread crumbs. Combine remaining ¾ cup (180 mL) of the water and the vinegar. Mix water-vinegar into flour until dough sticks together. Shape dough into ball. Knead on lightly floured surface 6 or 8 times. Cover with plastic wrap and let stand 20 minutes. Uncover and knead 4 or 5 times. Divide dough into 12 equal

portions. Shape each portion into a smooth ball.

4. Roll each ball of dough on lightly floured surface into a circle 5 to 6 inches (13 to 15 cm) in diameter. Brush around edges lightly with water. Spoon a heaping

tablespoon of pork mixture onto center of each circle. Carefully pinch edges together to seal dough around filling. Bring the two ends of dough over the seam and pinch together.

5. Cut waxed paper into twelve (5-inch or 13 cm) squares. Brush one side of paper lightly with oil. Place

a bun, seam side down, on each square.

6. Place buns with paper in single layer on steamer rack over boiling water. Cover and steam buns until done, about 20 minutes.

Makes 1 dozen

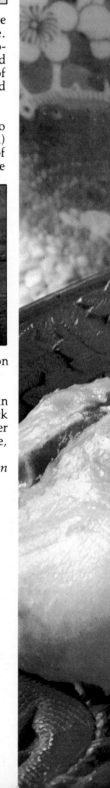

Ginger Beef

2½ tablespoons (37 mL) white vinegar
2 teaspoons (10 mL) sugar
½ teaspoon (2 mL) salt
4 ounces (115 g) fresh ginger root, pared and cut into thin slices
1 pound (450 g) beef tenderloin
2 tablespoons (30 mL) dry sherry
2 teaspoons (10 mL) cornstarch
1 teaspoon (5 mL) soy sauce
3 tablespoons (45 mL) vegetable oil
1 large green pepper
6 green onions
1 red chili pepper, cut into thin slices, if desired

1. Combine vinegar, sugar and salt in small glass or plastic bowl. Stir until sugar dissolves. Mix in ginger. Let stand 20 to 30 minutes, stirring occasionally.

2. Cut meat across the grain into thin slices about 1½ inches (4 cm) long. Combine sherry, cornstarch and soy sauce in medium glass or

plastic bowl. Mix in meat. Let stand 20 minutes, stirring occasionally.

3. Heat 2 tablespoons (30 mL) of the oil in wok over high heat. Add ⅓ of the meat, spreading slices out in wok so they do not overlap.

Cook until meat is brown, 2 to 3 minutes on each side. Remove meat from pan. Repeat procedure twice with remaining meat.

4. Remove seeds from green pepper. Cut green pepper into 1-inch (2.5 cm) pieces. Cut onions into 1-inch (2.5 cm) pieces.

5. Heat remaining 1 tablespoon (15 mL) oil in wok. Add pepper, onions and ginger mixture with marinade to wok. Stir-fry until vegetables are crisp-tender, 2 to 3 minutes. Return meat to wok. Cook and stir until hot throughout. Garnish with chili.

Makes 4 servings

Tenderloin Chinese Style

1 pound (450 g) beef tenderloin
3 tablespoons (45 mL) dry sherry
1½ tablespoons (22 mL) soy sauce
2 teaspoons (10 mL) oyster sauce
1 teaspoon (5 mL) sugar
1 teaspoon (5 mL) cornstarch
½ teaspoon (2 mL) baking soda
¼ teaspoon (1 mL) salt
1 clove garlic, crushed
1½ tablespoons (22 mL) vegetable oil
2 medium yellow onions, cut into thin slices

1. Remove and discard fat from meat. Cut meat across the grain into thin slices.

2. Combine sherry, soy sauce, oyster sauce, sugar, cornstarch, baking soda, salt and garlic in medium glass bowl. Mix in meat. Cover and refrigerate at least 3 hours.

3. Heat oil in wok over high heat. Stir-fry onions in the oil until golden, 3 to 5 minutes. Transfer onions to serving plate. Keep warm.

4. Add about ⅓ of the meat to wok, spreading out slices so they do not overlap. Cook slices on each side just until lightly browned, 2 to 3 minutes. Remove meat from pan and arrange over onion slices. Repeat twice to cook remaining meat.

Makes 4 servings

Beef with Peppers

1 ounce (30 g) dried
  mushrooms
Boiling water
1 pound (450 g) beef
  tenderloin
2 small yellow onions
1 green pepper
1 red pepper
2½ tablespoons (37 mL)
  vegetable oil
1 clove garlic, crushed
¼ teaspoon (1 mL) five-
  spice powder
¼ cup (60 mL) water
1 tablespoon (15 mL) soy
  sauce
1 teaspoon (5 mL)
  cornstarch
1 teaspoon (5 mL) instant
  beef bouillon granules
1 teaspoon (5 mL) sesame
  oil

1. Place mushrooms in a bowl and cover with boiling water. Let stand 30 minutes. Drain and squeeze dry. Remove and discard stems. Slice mushroom caps into thin strips.

2. Cut meat into thin slices 1 inch (2.5 cm) long. Cut onions into wedges. Remove seeds from peppers and cut peppers into thin slices.

3. Heat vegetable oil in wok over high heat. Add garlic and five-spice powder. Stir-fry 15 seconds. Add meat. Stir-fry until meat is brown, about 5 minutes. Add onions. Stir-fry 2 minutes. Add mushrooms and peppers. Stir-fry until peppers are crisp-tender, about 2 minutes.

4. Combine all remaining ingredients. Pour mixture over meat-vegetable mixture. Cook and stir until liquid boils and thickens.

Makes 4 servings

Beef with Celery

1 pound (450 g) beef rump
  or round steak
2 tablespoons (30 mL)
  soy sauce
1 teaspoon (5 mL) white
  vinegar
1 egg white
4 to 6 stalks celery
1½ cups (375 mL) water
½ teaspoon (2 mL) salt
3 tablespoons (45 mL)
  vegetable oil
6 green onions, cut into
  1-inch (2.5 cm) pieces
1 tablespoon (15 mL) finely
  chopped, pared fresh
  ginger root
1 clove garlic, crushed
1½ tablespoons (22 mL)
  dry sherry
1 tablespoon (15 mL)
  cornstarch
2 teaspoons (10 mL) oyster
  sauce

1. Cut meat across the grain into thin strips 1½ inches (4 cm) long. Combine ½ tablespoon (7 mL) of the soy sauce, vinegar and egg white in medium bowl; beat lightly with fork until foamy. Mix in meat. Cover and let stand 1 hour, stirring occasionally.

2. Cut celery into ½-inch (1.5 cm) diagonal slices. Combine celery, 1 cup (250 mL) of the water and the salt in saucepan. Cook over medium-high heat until boiling. Boil 3 minutes. Drain celery.

3. Heat 2 tablespoons (30 mL) of the oil in wok over high heat. Drain meat and add to wok. Stir-fry until meat is brown, about 5 minutes. Remove meat from wok.

4. Add remaining 1 tablespoon (15 mL) oil to wok. Add celery, onions, ginger and garlic. Stir-fry 1 minute. Return meat to wok; mix well.

5. Combine remaining ½ cup (125 mL) water, 1½ tablespoons (22 mL) soy sauce, the sherry, cornstarch and oyster sauce. Pour over meat-vegetable mixture. Cook and stir until liquid boils and thickens.

Makes 4 servings

Sweet and Sour Pork

2½ pounds (1125 g) lean pork chops
¼ cup (60 mL) soy sauce
1½ tablespoons (22 mL) dry sherry
2 teaspoons (10 mL) sugar
1 egg yolk
10 tablespoons (150 mL) cornstarch
3 cups (750 mL) vegetable oil
1 large yellow onion
8 green onions
1 red or green pepper
4 ounces (115 g) fresh mushrooms
2 stalks celery
1 medium cucumber
3 tablespoons (45 mL) vegetable oil
1 can (20 ounces or 565 g) pineapple chunks in syrup
¼ cup (60 mL) white vinegar
3 tablespoons (45 mL) tomato sauce
1 cup (250 mL) water

1. Trim chops, discarding fat and bones. Cut pork into 1-inch (2.5 cm) pieces. Mix soy sauce, sherry, sugar and egg yolk in large glass bowl. Mix in pork. Cover and let stand 1 hour, stirring occasionally.

2. Drain pork, reserving soy sauce mixture. Coat pork with 8 tablespoons (125 mL) of the cornstarch. Heat the 3 cups (750 mL) oil in wok over high heat until it reaches 375°F (190°C). Cook ½ of the pork in oil until brown, about 5 min-utes. Drain on absorbent paper. Cook and drain remaining pork.

3. Cut yellow onion into thin slices. Cut green onions into thin diagonal slices. Remove seeds from pepper and chop coarsely. Clean mushrooms and cut into halves or quarters. Cut celery into ½-inch (1.5 cm) diagonal slices. Cut cucumber lengthwise into quarters and remove seeds. Cut cucumber into ¼-inch (0.5 cm) wide pieces.

4. Heat the 3 tablespoons (45 mL) oil in wok over high heat. Add all the prepared vegetables to oil. Stir-fry 3 minutes. Drain pineapple, reserving syrup. Add the syrup, reserved soy sauce mixture, vinegar and to-mato sauce to vegetables. Combine water and remain-ing 2 tablespoons (30 mL) cornstarch. Add to vegeta-bles. Cook and stir until sauce boils and thickens. Add pork and pineapple. Cook and stir until hot throughout.

Makes 6 servings

Spiced Pork

3 pounds (1350 g) lean pork chops
2 tablespoons (30 mL) cornstarch
3 tablespoons (45 mL) soy sauce
2 tablespoons (30 mL) sweet sherry
1 teaspoon (5 mL) grated pared fresh ginger root
½ teaspoon (2 mL) five-spice powder
⅛ teaspoon (0.5 mL) pepper
3 cups (750 mL) vegetable oil
¼ cup (60 mL) water
1 teaspoon (5 mL) instant chicken bouillon granules
Chinese Mixed Pickles (see Index for page number), if desired

1. Trim chops, discarding fat and bones. Mix corn-starch, 2 tablespoons (30 mL) of the soy sauce, the sherry, ginger, five-spice powder and pepper. Add pork, one piece at a time, to cornstarch mixture, turning

to coat completely. Cover and let stand 1 to 2 hours, stirring occasionally.

2. Heat oil in wok over high heat until it reaches 375°F (190°C). Cook ½ of the pork in oil until brown and cooked through, 3 to 5 minutes. Drain on absor-bent paper. Cook and drain remaining pork.

3. Cut pork into slices ¼ to ½ inch (0.5 to 1.5 cm) wide. Transfer pork to serving dish. Keep warm.

4. Combine water, bouillon and remaining 1 tablespoon (15 mL) soy sauce in small saucepan. Heat until mix-ture boils. Pour mixture over sliced pork. Garnish with Chinese Mixed Pickles.

Makes 4 servings

Curried Beef

1 pound (450 g) beef
   tenderloin
2 medium yellow onions
2 medium potatoes
3½ tablespoons (52 mL)
   vegetable oil
4 teaspoons (20 mL) curry
   powder
⅓ cup (80 mL) water
1 tablespoon (15 mL)
   cornstarch
2 tablespoons (30 mL) satay
   sauce
1½ tablespoons (22 mL)
   soy sauce
1½ tablespoons (22 mL)
   dry sherry
1 tablespoon (15 mL)
   Chinese chili sauce
1 teaspoon (5 mL) instant
   chicken bouillon
   granules
Steamed Rice (see Index for
   page number), if desired

1. Remove and discard fat from meat. Cut meat across the grain into thin slices. Peel onions, cut into wedges and separate layers. Pare potatoes and cut into ½-inch (1.5 cm) cubes.

2. Heat 2½ tablespoons (37 mL) of the oil in wok over high heat. Stir-fry potatoes in oil until crisp-tender, about 5 minutes. Add onions and 2 teaspoons (10 mL) of the curry powder. Stir-fry 2 minutes. Remove mixture from wok.

3. Heat remaining 1 tablespoon (15 mL) oil in wok over high heat. Stir-fry meat until light brown, 3 to 4 minutes. Add potato mixture.

4. Combine remaining 2 teaspoons (10 mL) curry powder and all other remaining ingredients. Pour over meat-potato mixture. Cook and stir until liquid boils. Reduce heat and simmer 3 minutes. Serve with rice.

Makes 4 servings

Beef Chow Mein

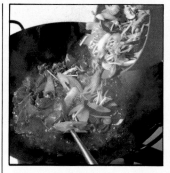

1½ pounds (675 g) beef
   rump steak
3½ tablespoons (52 mL)
   soy sauce
3½ tablespoons (52 mL)
   dry sherry
1 tablespoon (15 mL) satay
   sauce
3 stalks celery
2 medium yellow onions
4 ounces (115 g) fresh
   mushrooms
1 red or green pepper
4 ounces (115 g) bean
   sprouts
12 ounces (340 g)
   Chinese egg noodles
4 tablespoons (60 mL)
   vegetable oil
¾ cup (180 mL) water
1 tablespoon (15 mL)
   cornstarch
2½ tablespoons (37 mL)
   oyster sauce
2 teaspoons (10 mL) instant
   chicken bouillon
   granules

1. Remove and discard fat from meat. Cut meat across the grain into thin slices. Combine 1½ tablespoons (22 mL) of the soy sauce, 1 tablespoon (15 mL) of the sherry and the satay sauce in glass bowl. Mix in meat. Cover and let stand 1 hour.

2. Cut celery into ½-inch (1.5 cm) diagonal slices. Peel onions, cut into wedges and separate layers. Clean and slice mushrooms. Remove seeds from pepper and cut pepper into thin strips. Rinse sprouts and drain.

3. Cook noodles until tender according to package directions. Drain well. Heat 1 tablespoon (15 mL) of the oil in wok over medium-high heat. Add noodles and 1 tablespoon (15 mL) of the remaining soy sauce. Stir-fry until noodles are light brown, 2 minutes. Place noodles on serving plate. Keep warm.

4. Blend water, cornstarch, oyster sauce, bouillon, remaining 2½ tablespoons (37 mL) sherry and 1 tablespoon (15 mL) soy sauce.

5. Heat 1 tablespoon (15 mL) of the remaining oil in wok over high heat. Stir-fry onions in oil 1 minute. Add celery, mushrooms, pepper and sprouts. Stir-fry 2 minutes. Remove vegetables from wok.

6. Heat remaining 2 tablespoons (30 mL) oil in wok over high heat. Add meat and stir-fry until meat is brown, about 5 minutes. Stir in water mixture. Cover and cook 3 minutes.

7. Return vegetables to wok. Cook and stir until hot throughout, 1 to 2 minutes longer. Spoon mixture over noodles.

Makes 4 to 6 servings

POULTRY

Lemon Chicken

CHICKEN
4 whole chicken breasts
½ cup (125 mL) cornstarch
½ teaspoon (2 mL) salt
⅛ teaspoon (0.5 mL) pepper
¼ cup (60 mL) water
4 egg yolks, slightly beaten
3 cups (750 mL) vegetable oil
4 green onions, sliced

LEMON SAUCE
1½ cups (375 mL) water
½ cup (125 mL) lemon juice
3½ tablespoons (52 mL) packed light brown sugar
3 tablespoons (45 mL) cornstarch
3 tablespoons (45 mL) honey
2 teaspoons (10 mL) instant chicken bouillon granules
1 teaspoon (5 mL) grated pared fresh ginger root

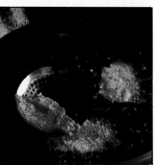

3. Pour oil into wok. Heat over high heat until oil reaches 375°F (190°C). Dip chicken breasts, one at a time, into cornstarch-egg yolk mixture. Fry breasts, two or three at a time, in hot oil until golden, about 5 minutes. Drain breasts on absorbent paper. Keep warm while cooking remaining chicken.

4. Cut each breast into three or four pieces and arrange on serving plate. Sprinkle with onions.

For Chicken
1. Remove skin from chicken and discard. Cut breasts in half. Remove and discard bones. Pound chicken breasts lightly with mallet or rolling pin.

2. Combine cornstarch, salt and pepper in small bowl. Gradually blend in water and egg yolks.

For Sauce
5. Combine all ingredients in medium saucepan. Stir until blended. Cook over medium heat, stirring constantly, until sauce boils and thickens, about 5 minutes. Pour over chicken.
Makes 4 to 6 servings

Sesame Chicken Salad

1 tablespoon (15 mL) sesame seeds
3 whole chicken breasts
6 cups (1.5 L) water
2 tablespoons (30 mL) soy sauce
½ teaspoon (2 mL) salt
½ teaspoon (2 mL) five-spice powder
3 stalks celery
1 tablespoon (15 mL) sesame oil
1 tablespoon (15 mL) vegetable oil
¼ teaspoon (1 mL) ground ginger
⅛ teaspoon (0.5 mL) pepper

1. Sprinkle sesame seeds into small, shallow baking pan or cookie sheet with sides. Bake in preheated 350°F (180°C) oven until golden, 5 to 8 minutes.

2. Combine chicken, water, 1 tablespoon (15 mL) of the soy sauce, the salt and five-spice powder in 3 or 4-quart (3 or 4 L) saucepan. Cover and cook over high heat until water boils. Reduce heat and simmer 15 to 20 minutes. Remove from heat. Let chicken stand in water 1 hour.

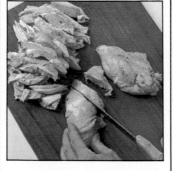

3. Remove chicken from water (reserve water) and drain. Remove and discard chicken bones. Cut meat into ½-inch (1.5 cm) wide slices.

4. Cut celery into diagonal slices. Heat reserved water over high heat until it boils. Add celery and cook until crisp-tender, 1 to 2 minutes. Drain celery well.

5. Combine remaining 1 tablespoon (15 mL) soy sauce with oils, ginger and pepper in large bowl. Add chicken and celery. Toss until completely combined. Transfer mixture to serving dish. Sprinkle with sesame seeds.

Makes 4 servings

How to Chop Chicken Chinese Style

Recipes for Chinese chicken dishes often instruct that chicken be cut into serving-size pieces. These pieces should be smaller than chicken pieces generally are cut. Here are the directions for cutting a whole chicken Chinese style. A cleaver is the best utensil for chopping a chicken, although a sharp knife, kitchen or poultry shears may be used.

1. Place chicken, breast side up, on a heavy cutting board. Cut the chicken in half lengthwise, cutting slightly to one side of each the breast bone and the back bone. Cut completely through the chicken to make two pieces. Remove and discard the backbone, if desired.

2. Pull each leg up slightly from the breast section. Cut through the ball and socket joint to remove each leg.

3. Cut through the knee joint of each leg to separate into a drumstick and thigh. Pull each wing away from breast and cut through the joint next to the breast.

4. Cut each drumstick, thigh and breast piece crosswise into three pieces, cutting completely through bones. Cut each wing into two pieces.

Makes 22 small serving-size pieces

Honey Chili Chicken

1 broiler-fryer chicken
(about 3 pounds or
1350 g)
½ cup (125 mL) all-
purpose flour
½ teaspoon (2 mL) salt
3 cups (750 mL) vegetable
oil
⅓ cup (80 mL) water
⅓ cup (80 mL) lemon juice
2 teaspoons (10 mL)
cornstarch
4 teaspoons (20 mL)
Chinese chili sauce
2 teaspoons (10 mL) soy
sauce
1½ teaspoons (7 mL)
grated pared fresh ginger
root
3 tablespoons (45 mL)
honey
6 green onions, cut into
thin lengthwise slices

1. Remove giblets from chicken. Rinse chicken and cut into small serving-size pieces. Combine flour and salt. Coat chicken pieces with flour mixture.

2. Heat oil in wok over high heat until it reaches 375°F (190°C). Add chicken pieces, one at a time, to hot oil (cook only ⅓ of the pieces at a time). Cook until golden, about 5 minutes. Drain on absorbent paper. Repeat with remaining chicken.

3. Pour all but 1 tablespoon (15 mL) of the oil out of wok. Combine water, lemon juice, cornstarch, chili sauce and soy sauce.

4. Add ginger to oil in wok. Stir-fry 1 minute. Add honey to ginger. Cook and stir 1 minute. Add corn-starch-chili mixture to honey and ginger. Cook and stir until mixture boils, about 1 minute.

5. Stir chicken pieces into chili mixture. Cook and stir until chicken is hot through-out, about 3 minutes. Stir in onions. Cook and stir 1 minute.

Makes 4 to 6 servings

Chicken with Lychees

3 whole chicken breasts
6 green onions
1 red pepper
¼ cup (60 mL)
cornstarch
3 tablespoons (45 mL)
vegetable oil
½ cup (125 mL) tomato
sauce
½ cup (125 mL) water
2 teaspoons (10 mL) instant
chicken bouillon
granules
1 teaspoon (5 mL) sugar
1 teaspoon (5 mL)
cornstarch
1 can (11 ounces or 310 g)
whole peeled lychees,
drained
Vermicelli, cooked and
drained (see Index for
page number), if desired

1. Cut chicken breasts in half. Remove and discard bones. Cut each breast half into six pieces. Cut onions into 1-inch (2.5 cm) pieces. Remove seeds from pepper; cut pepper into 1-inch (2.5 cm) pieces.

2. Measure ¼ cup (60 mL) cornstarch into large bowl. Add chicken pieces and toss until well coated.

3. Heat oil in wok over high heat. Add chicken. Stir-fry

until chicken is light brown, 5 to 8 minutes. Add onions and pepper to chicken. Stir-fry 1 minute.

4. Combine tomato sauce, ¼ cup of the water, the sugar and bouillon. Pour over chicken-vegetable mixture. Mix well. Stir in lychees. Cover, reduce heat to medium and cook until chicken is tender, about 5 minutes.

5. Combine remaining ¼ cup (60 mL) water and the 1 teaspoon (5 mL) cornstarch. Stir into chicken mixture. Cook and stir until mixture boils and thickens. Serve with Vermicelli.

Makes 4 servings

Chicken with Water Chestnuts

1 ounce (30 g) dried
  mushrooms
Boiling water
3 stalks celery
1 red or green pepper
1 medium yellow onion
1 can (8 ounces or 225 g)
  water chestnuts
8 ounces (225 g) bean
  sprouts
1 piece (about 1-inch or 2.5
  cm square) fresh ginger
  root
2 whole chicken breasts
⅔ cup (160 mL) water
4 teaspoons (20 mL)
  cornstarch
1 tablespoon (15 mL)
  instant chicken bouillon
  granules
1 tablespoon (15 mL) dry
  sherry
1 tablespoon (15 mL) soy
  sauce
1 tablespoon (15 mL) oyster
  sauce
1½ cups (375 mL)
  vegetable oil

1. Place mushrooms in bowl and cover with boiling water. Let stand 30 minutes. Drain and squeeze excess liquid from mushrooms. Cut mushrooms into halves.

2. Cut celery into ½-inch (1.5 cm) slices. Remove seeds from pepper and cut pepper into thin strips. Peel

onion, cut into wedges and separate layers. Drain water chestnuts and cut into halves. Rinse sprouts with water and drain. Pare ginger and cut into thin slices.

3. Remove skin and bones from chicken and discard. Cut chicken into 1-inch (2.5 cm) pieces.

4. Combine water, cornstarch, bouillon, sherry, soy sauce and oyster sauce.

5. Heat oil in wok over high heat until it reaches 375°F (190°C). Cook chicken pieces in the oil until golden, 5 minutes. Drain on absorbent paper.

6. Remove all but 2 tablespoons (30 mL) oil from wok. Add celery, pepper, onion, water chestnuts, bean sprouts, ginger and chicken to wok. Toss lightly until combined.

7. Pour water mixture over vegetable-chicken mixture. Cook and stir until vegetables are crisp-tender, 3 to 5 minutes.
Makes 4 servings

Marinated Chicken Wings

3 tablespoons (45 mL) soy
  sauce
3 tablespoons (45 mL) dry
  sherry
2 tablespoons (30 mL) light
  brown sugar
1 teaspoon (5 mL) grated
  pared fresh ginger root
2 cloves garlic, crushed
6 green onions
1½ pounds (675 g) chicken
  wings
2 tablespoons (30 mL)
  vegetable oil
1 can (8 ounces or 225 g)
  sliced bamboo shoots
4 teaspoons (20 mL)
  cornstarch
¾ cup (180 mL) water
1 teaspoon (5 mL) instant
  chicken bouillon
  granules

1. Combine soy sauce, sherry, sugar, ginger and garlic in large glass bowl. Cut onions into thin diagonal slices. Add onions and chicken to soy sauce mixture. Toss to coat completely. Cover and let stand 1 hour, stirring occasionally.

2. Heat oil in wok over high heat. Drain bamboo shoots and stir-fry in oil 2 minutes. Remove from wok.

3. Drain chicken and onions, reserving soy sauce mixture. Place chicken and onions in wok. Cook over medium-high heat until chicken is brown on both sides, about 5 minutes. Reduce heat to low. Cook until chicken is tender, 15 to 20 minutes.

4. Measure cornstarch into small bowl. Blend in a few tablespoons of the water until smooth. Add remaining water, the bouillon and reserved soy sauce mixture. Pour mixture over chicken. Cook over high heat until liquid boils and thickens. Stir in bamboo shoots. Cook and stir 2 minutes.
Makes 4 servings

Spiced Chicken

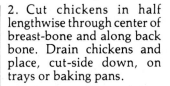

2 broiler-fryer chickens (about 3 pounds or 1350 g each)
Water
1 cup (250 mL) soy sauce
1 piece fresh ginger root (2x1-inches or 5x2.5 cm), pared and shredded
2 cloves garlic, crushed
4½ teaspoons (22 mL) five-spice powder
3 tablespoons (45 mL) dry sherry
3 tablespoons (45 mL) honey
1½ tablespoons (22 mL) soy sauce
½ teaspoon (2 mL) sesame oil
3 cups (750 mL) vegetable oil

FRIED SALT AND PEPPER
¼ cup (60 mL) salt
½ teaspoon (2 mL) pepper
1 teaspoon (5 mL) five-spice powder

1. Remove giblets from chickens and reserve for another use. Rinse chickens and place in large stock pot or kettle. Add enough water to cover chickens, 1 cup (250 mL) soy sauce, the ginger, garlic and 4 teaspoons (20 mL) five-spice powder. Cover and cook over high heat until water boils. Reduce heat and simmer five minutes. Turn off heat. Allow chickens to stand in liquid until liquid cools to lukewarm. Drain chickens.

2. Cut chickens in half lengthwise through center of breast-bone and along back bone. Drain chickens and place, cut-side down, on trays or baking pans.

3. Combine sherry, honey, 1½ tablespoons (22 mL) soy sauce, the remaining ½ teaspoon (2 mL) five-spice powder and sesame oil in small bowl. Brush or rub all of the mixture over chickens.

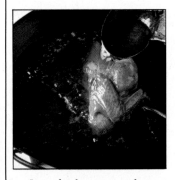

4. Let chickens stand two hours, brushing occasionally with soy mixture.

5. Heat 3 cups (750 mL) vegetable oil in wok over high heat until it reaches 375°F (190°C). Cook ½ of a chicken at a time in hot oil until brown, 2 to 3 minutes on each side. Drain on absorbent paper. Cut each half into serving-size pieces.

6. For Fried Salt and Pepper, combine salt and pepper in skillet. Cook over medium heat 2 minutes. Stir in five-spice powder. Cook 1 minute longer. Divide between small dishes and serve as a dip for chicken.

Makes 8 servings

Chicken with Mangoes

1 cup (250 mL) all-purpose flour
1¾ cups (430 mL) water
½ teaspoon (2 mL) salt
¼ teaspoon (1 mL) baking powder
3 whole chicken breasts
1 piece fresh ginger root (2x1-inches or 5x2.5 cm)
8 green onions
1 can (15 ounces or 425 g) mangoes
3 cups (750 mL) vegetable oil
3 tablespoons (45 mL) white vinegar
3 tablespoons (45 mL) dry sherry
4 teaspoons (20 mL) soy sauce
2 teaspoons (10 mL) sugar
2 teaspoons (10 mL) cornstarch
2 teaspoons (10 mL) instant chicken bouillon granules
1 teaspoon (5 mL) sesame oil

1. Combine flour, 1 cup (250 mL) of the water, the salt and baking powder. Beat with whisk until blended. Let stand 15 minutes.

2. Remove skin and bones from chicken and discard. Cut chicken into ¼-inch (1 cm) wide strips. Mix strips into flour mixture.

3. Pare ginger and cut into wafer-thin slices. Cut onions into ½-inch (1.5 cm) pieces. Drain mangoes and cut into ½-inch wide (1.5 cm) strips.

4. Heat vegetable oil in wok over high heat until it reaches 375°F (190°C). Add chicken, one strip at a time, to hot oil (cook only ¼ of the chicken at a time). Cook until golden, 3 to 5 minutes. Drain on absorbent paper. Repeat to cook remaining chicken.

5. Remove all but 1 tablespoon (15 mL) oil from wok. Reduce heat to medium. Add ginger to oil in wok. Stir-fry until ginger is light brown, about 2 minutes.

6. Combine remaining ¾ cup (180 mL) water, the vinegar, sherry, soy sauce, sugar, cornstarch, bouillon and sesame oil. Carefully add to ginger all at once. Cook and stir until mixture boils. Add onions. Reduce heat and simmer 3 minutes.

7. Mix chicken and mangoes into soy sauce mixture. Cook and stir 2 minutes. Serve immediately.
Makes 4 to 6 servings

Almond Chicken

1½ cups (375 mL) water
4 tablespoons (60 mL) dry sherry
2½ tablespoons (37 mL) cornstarch
4 teaspoons (20 mL) soy sauce
1 teaspoon (5 mL) instant chicken bouillon granules
4 whole chicken breasts
1 egg white
½ teaspoon (2 mL) salt
1 large carrot
6 green onions
3 stalks celery
8 fresh mushrooms, sliced
3 cups (750 mL) vegetable oil
½ cup (125 mL) blanched whole almonds (about 3 ounces or 85 g)
1 teaspoon (5 mL) grated fresh ginger root
½ cup (125 mL) drained, sliced bamboo shoots (½ of 8 ounce or 225 g can)

1. Combine water, 2 tablespoons (30 mL) of the sherry, 1½ tablespoons (22 mL) of the cornstarch, the soy sauce and bouillon in small saucepan. Cook and stir over medium heat until mixture boils and thickens, about 5 minutes. Keep warm.

2. Remove skin and bones from chicken. Cut chicken into 1-inch (2.5 cm) pieces.

Combine remaining 2 tablespoons (30 mL) sherry, 1 tablespoon (15 mL) cornstarch, egg white and salt. Mix in chicken pieces.

3. Pare carrot and dice. Cut onions into 1-inch (2.5 cm) pieces. Cut celery diagonally into ½-inch (1.5 cm) slices.

4. Heat oil in wok over high heat until it reaches 375°F (190°C). Add chicken pieces, one at a time, to hot oil (cook only ⅓ of the pieces at a time). Cook until light brown, 3 to 5 minutes.

Drain on absorbent paper. Repeat with remaining chicken.

5. Remove all but 2 tablespoons (30 mL) oil from wok. Stir-fry almonds in the oil until golden, about 2 minutes. Drain.

6. Add carrot and ginger to wok. Stir-fry 1 minute. Add all remaining vegetables. Stir-fry until crisp-tender, about 3 minutes. Mix in chicken, almonds and sauce. Stir-fry until hot.
Makes 4 to 6 servings

Ginger Green Onion Chicken

1 broiler-fryer chicken
(about 3 pounds or
1350 g)
1 piece fresh ginger root
(2x1-inches or 5x2.5
cm), cut into thin slices
1¼ teaspoons (6 mL) salt
½ teaspoon (2 mL) pepper
Water
⅓ cup (80 mL) vegetable
oil
8 green onions, finely
chopped
3 tablespoons (45 mL)
grated pared fresh ginger
root
2 teaspoons (10 mL) white
vinegar
1 teaspoon (5 mL) soy
sauce
Steamed Rice (see Index for
page number)

1. Remove giblets from chicken and reserve for another use. Rinse chicken and place in large saucepan or Dutch oven. Add sliced ginger, 1 teaspoon (5 mL) of the salt, ¼ teaspoon (1 mL) of the pepper and enough water to cover chicken. Cover and bring to boil over high heat. Reduce heat and simmer until tender, about 40 minutes. Let chicken stand in water until cool.

2. Drain chicken and refrigerate until cold. Cut chicken into serving-size pieces (see page 42).

3. Combine remaining ¼ teaspoon (1 mL) salt and ¼ teaspoon (1 mL) pepper with remaining ingredients in a jar with lid. Cover jar and shake well. Refrigerate 1 to 2 hours.

4. Place chicken pieces in serving bowl. Shake oil-ginger mixture and pour over chicken. Serve with Steamed Rice.
Makes 4 to 6 servings

Beggar's Chicken

1 broiler-fryer chicken
(about 3 pounds or
1350 g)
6½ tablespoons (97 mL)
soy sauce
2½ tablespoons (37 mL)
vegetable oil
2½ tablespoons (37 mL)
dry sherry
1 teaspoon (5 mL) sugar
¼ teaspoon (1 mL) five-
spice powder
4 green onions, finely
chopped
1 piece fresh ginger root
(about 1-inch or 2.5 cm
square), pared and cut
into thin slices
4 cups (1 L) all-purpose
flour
3 cups (750 mL) salt
(2 pounds or 900 g)
1½ cups (375 mL) water
(approximately)

1. Remove giblets from chicken and reserve for another use. Rinse chicken and pat dry with paper toweling. Place chicken on large piece of greased extra-wide, heavy duty aluminum foil. Rub or brush 2½ tablespoons (37 mL) of the soy sauce completely over chicken. Rub or brush the oil completely over chicken.

Pull skin at neck end under chicken and secure with small skewer. Tuck wing tips under chicken.

2. Combine remaining 4 tablespoons (60 mL) soy sauce, the sherry, sugar, five-spice powder, onions and ginger. Pour mixture into cavity of chicken, holding tail end of chicken up slightly so liquid does not run out of cavity. Secure tail end of chicken with small skewers. Wrap foil around chicken, sealing securely.

3. Combine flour and salt in bowl. Gradually mix in enough water to make a firm dough. Roll out dough on lightly floured surface until about ¼-inch (0.5 cm) thick (dough must be large enough to completely cover chicken).

4. Place foil-wrapped chicken onto center of dough. Fold dough over chicken, pressing edges and ends together to seal completely. Place chicken in well-greased 13x9x2-inch (33x23x5 cm) baking pan.

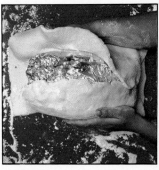

5. Bake chicken in pre-heated 450°F (230°C) oven 1 hour. Reduce heat to 300°F (150°C). Bake 2½ hours longer.

6. Remove chicken from oven. Using mallet or hammer, break pastry. Remove chicken from pastry and place on serving plate. Carefully remove foil and skewers.
Makes 4 servings

Hoi Sin Chicken

8 ounces (225 g) fresh broccoli
2 medium yellow onions
1 red or green pepper
2 cans (4 ounces or 115 g each) whole button mushrooms
1 broiler-fryer chicken (3 pounds or 1350 g)
½ cup (125 mL) cornstarch
3 cups (750 mL) vegetable oil
2 teaspoons (10 mL) grated pared fresh ginger root
1 cup (250 mL) water
1 tablespoon (15 mL) cornstarch
3 tablespoons (45 mL) dry sherry
3 tablespoons (45 mL) cider vinegar
3 tablespoons (45 mL) hoi sin sauce
4 teaspoons (20 mL) soy sauce
2 teaspoons (10 mL) instant chicken bouillon granules

1. Wash broccoli and cut into 1-inch (2.5 cm) pieces. Peel and chop onions. Remove seeds from pepper and chop pepper coarsely. Drain mushrooms.

2. Remove giblets from chicken and reserve for another use. Rinse chicken and cut into serving-size pieces (see page 42). Coat chicken pieces with ½ cup (125 mL) cornstarch.

3. Heat vegetable oil in wok over high heat until it reaches 375°F (190°C). Add chicken pieces, one at a time, to hot oil (cook only ⅓ of the pieces at a time). Cook until golden and completely cooked, about 5 minutes.

Drain on absorbent paper. Repeat with remaining chicken.

4. Remove all but 2 tablespoons (30 mL) of the oil from wok. Stir-fry ginger in the oil over medium heat 1 minute. Add onion to ginger. Stir-fry over high heat 1 minute. Add broccoli, pepper and mushrooms. Stir-fry 2 minutes.

5. Combine water and all remaining ingredients. Add to vegetable mixture. Cook and stir until liquid boils and becomes translucent.

6. Return chicken to wok. Cook and stir until chicken is hot throughout, 2 minutes.
Makes 6 servings

Chicken Chow Mein

Fried Noodles (see Index for page number)
2 whole chicken breasts
8 ounces (225 g) uncooked boneless lean pork
2½ tablespoons (37 mL) dry sherry
2 tablespoons (30 mL) soy sauce
3 teaspoons (15 mL) cornstarch
2 medium yellow onions
1 red or green pepper
2 stalks celery
8 green onions
4 ounces (115 g) cabbage (¼ of small head)
1 piece fresh ginger root (1 inch or 2.5 cm square)
8 ounces (225 g) uncooked medium shrimp
2 tablespoons (30 mL) vegetable oil
1 clove garlic, crushed
½ cup (125 mL) water
2 teaspoons (10 mL) instant chicken bouillon granules

1. Prepare Fried Noodles.

2. Remove skin and bones from chicken and discard. Cut chicken and pork into 1-inch (2.5 cm) pieces. Blend ½ tablespoon (7 mL) each of the sherry and soy sauce and 1 teaspoon (5 mL) of the cornstarch in large bowl. Mix in chicken and pork. Cover and let stand 1 hour.

3. Peel and chop yellow onions. Remove seeds from pepper and cut pepper into thin slices. Cut celery into 1-inch (2.5 cm) diagonal slices. Chop green onions. Shred cabbage. Pare ginger and chop finely. Remove shells and back veins from shrimp.

4. Heat oil in wok over high heat. Stir-fry ginger and garlic in the oil for 1 minute. Add chicken and pork. Stir-fry over high heat until pork is no longer pink, 5 minutes.

5. Add shrimp to chicken mixture. Stir-fry until shrimp is done, 3 minutes longer.

6. Add all prepared vegetables to chicken mixture. Cook and stir until vegetables are crisp-tender, 3 to 5 minutes.

7. Combine water, bouillon, remaining 2 teaspoons (10 mL) cornstarch, 2 tablespoons (30 mL) sherry and 1½ tablespoons (22 mL) soy sauce. Pour mixture over chicken-vegetable mixture in wok. Cook and stir until sauce boils and thickens. Cook and stir 1 minute longer.

8. Arrange noodles on serving plate. Spoon Chow Mein over noodles.
Makes 6 servings

Combination Chop Suey

2 whole chicken breasts, cooked
½ head Chinese cabbage (about 8 ounces or 225 g)
4 ounces (115 g) fresh green beans
3 stalks celery
2 medium yellow onions
1 large carrot
8 ounces (225 g) uncooked medium or small shrimp
8 ounces (225 g) uncooked boneless lean pork
3 tablespoons (45 mL) vegetable oil
1 cup (250 mL) water
2 teaspoons (10 mL) cornstarch
1 teaspoon (5 mL) instant chicken bouillon granules
4 teaspoons (20 mL) soy sauce
1 can (8 ounces or 225 g) sliced bamboo shoots, drained

1. Remove skin and bones from cooked chicken. Coarsely chop chicken meat. Shred cabbage. Trim beans and cut into ½-inch (1.5 cm) diagonal slices. Cut celery into ½-inch (1.5 cm) diagonal slices. Chop onions. Pare carrot and chop finely. Remove shells and back veins from shrimp. Chop pork finely.

2. Heat oil in wok over high heat. Stir-fry pork in oil until brown, 5 minutes. Remove pork from wok.

3. Add cabbage, beans, celery, onions and carrot to wok. Stir-fry until vegetables are crisp-tender, about 3 minutes.

4. Combine water, cornstarch, bouillon and soy sauce. Pour mixture over vegetables. Cook and stir until liquid boils and thickens, about 3 minutes. Add chicken, shrimp and bamboo shoots. Cook and stir until shrimp is done, 3 minutes longer.

Makes 4 to 6 servings

Honeyed Chicken and Pineapple

1 broiler-fryer chicken (about 3 pounds or 1350 g)
½ cup (125 mL) cornstarch
3 cups (750 mL) vegetable oil
2 teaspoons (10 mL) grated, pared fresh ginger root
1 clove garlic, crushed
1 can (20 ounces or 565 g) pineapple chunks, drained
1 red or green pepper, seeded and cut into thin slices
1½ cups (375 mL) water
2 teaspoons (10 mL) cornstarch
1½ tablespoons (22 mL) honey
1 tablespoon (15 mL) instant chicken bouillon granules
1 teaspoon (5 mL) sesame oil
4 green onions, cut into thin slices

1. Remove giblets from chicken. Rinse chicken and cut into serving-size pieces (see page 42). Coat chicken pieces with ½ cup (125 mL) cornstarch.

2. Heat vegetable oil in wok over high heat until it reaches 375°F (190°C). Add chicken pieces, one at a time, to hot oil (cook only ⅓ of the pieces at a time). Cook until golden and completely cooked, about 5 minutes. Drain on absorbent paper. Repeat with remaining chicken.

3. Pour all but 2 tablespoons (30 mL) of the oil out of wok. Stir-fry ginger and garlic in the oil over medium heat 1 minute. Add drained pineapple and the sliced pepper to ginger mixture. Stir-fry over high heat 2 minutes. Remove from wok.

4. Mix water and remaining 2 teaspoons (10 mL) cornstarch. Blend in honey, bouillon and sesame oil. Pour mixture into wok. Cook and stir over high heat until mixture boils and thickens. Return chicken and pineapple-pepper mixture to wok. Cook and stir over high heat until hot throughout. Add green onions. Cook and stir 1 minute longer.

Makes 4 servings

Braised Duck

1 ready-to-cook duck
  (4 to 5 pounds or 1800 to
  2250 g)
10 tablespoons (150 mL)
  cornstarch
3 cups (750 mL) vegetable
  oil
2 cloves garlic, crushed
2 tablespoons (30 mL) dry
  sherry
2 tablespoons (30 mL) soy
  sauce
1 teaspoon (5 mL) grated
  pared fresh ginger root
2¾ cups (680 mL) water
2 teaspoons (10 mL) instant
  chicken bouillon
  granules
1 ounce (30 g) dried
  mushrooms
Boiling water
1 can (8 ounces or 225 g)
  sliced bamboo shoots
1 can (8 ounces or 225 g)
  water chestnuts
5 green onions
1½ teaspoons (7 mL) sugar
¼ teaspoon (1 mL) pepper

1. Rinse duck and cut into serving-size pieces (see page 42). Coat pieces with 8 tablespoons (120 mL) of the cornstarch.

2. Heat the vegetable oil in wok over high heat until it reaches 375°F (190°C). Add garlic and ¼ of the duck pieces, one at a time, to hot oil. Cook until brown, about 5 minutes. Drain duck on absorbent paper. Repeat to cook remaining duck pieces.

3. Remove oil from wok. Return duck to wok. Combine sherry, 1 tablespoon (15 mL) of the soy sauce and ginger. Pour mixture over duck. Cook and stir over high heat 2 minutes. Add 2 cups (500 mL) of the water and the bouillon. Cook until mixture boils. Transfer duck and liquid to large saucepan. Cover pan tightly and simmer duck over low heat until tender, about 1 hour.

4. Meanwhile, place mushrooms in bowl and cover with boiling water. Let stand 30 minutes. Drain mushrooms and squeeze out excess water. Remove and discard stems. Cut mushroom caps into thin slices.

5. Drain bamboo shoots and water chestnuts. Cut chestnuts into slices. Cut onions into thin diagonal slices.

6. Add mushrooms, bamboo shoots and water chestnuts to duck. Cook, stirring frequently, 5 minutes longer.

7. Skim off fat from liquid. Blend remaining ¾ cup (180 mL) water, 2 tablespoons (30 mL) cornstarch, 1 tablespoon (15 mL) soy sauce, the sugar, and pepper. Stir mixture into duck mixture. Cook and stir over medium heat until liquid thickens and boils, about 4 minutes. Transfer duck and liquid to serving bowl. Sprinkle with onion slices.

Makes 6 servings

Duck with Pineapple

1 ready-to-cook duck
  (4 to 5 pounds or 1800 to
  2250 g)
1¼ cups (310 mL) water
6 tablespoons (90 mL) dry
  sherry
4½ tablespoons (67 mL)
  white vinegar
4½ tablespoons (67 mL)
  soy sauce
4 tablespoons (60 mL)
  American-style barbecue
  sauce
¼ teaspoon (1 mL) five-
  spice powder
1 small ripe pineapple
4 green onions, if desired
2 tablespoons (30 mL)
  vegetable oil
2 teaspoons (10 mL) grated
  pared fresh ginger root
1 clove garlic, crushed
1 tablespoon (15 mL)
  cornstarch
Green Onion Curls
  (see Index for page
  number)

1. Rinse duck and place on rack in baking pan. Combine ½ cup (125 mL) of the water, 3 tablespoons (30 mL) each of the sherry, vinegar, soy sauce and barbecue sauce, and the ¼ teaspoon (1 mL) five-spice powder. Pour mixture over duck. Roast duck uncovered in preheated 425°F (220°C) oven, basting and turning frequently, until light brown, about 20 minutes. Reduce oven temperature to 350°F (180°C) and roast duck, basting and turning frequently, 1 hour longer.

Remove duck from oven. Cool completely.

2. Cut duck in half. Remove and discard backbone. Cut duck into small serving-size pieces.

3. Remove top leaves and all skin from pineapple. Cut pineapple into quarters. Cut out and discard core. Cut pineapple quarters crosswise into ¼-inch (0.5 cm) slices. Cut onions into thin diagonal slices.

4. Heat oil in wok over high heat. Stir-fry ginger and

garlic in the oil 1 minute. Add duck and stir-fry until duck is hot throughout, 3 to 4 minutes. Combine remaining ¾ cup (180 mL) water, 3 tablespoons (45 mL) sherry, 1½ tablespoons (22 mL) each vinegar and soy sauce, 1 tablespoon (15 mL) barbecue sauce and the cornstarch. Pour mixture over duck. Cook and stir until liquid boils. Add pineapple pieces and onions. Cook and stir until pineapple is hot, about 2 minutes longer. Garnish with Green Onion Curls.

Makes 6 servings

Barbecued Shrimp

1 pound (450 g) fresh large
  shrimp
1 egg white
2 teaspoons (10 mL)
  cornstarch
1 teaspoon (5 mL) salt
1 cup (250 mL) vegetable
  oil
1 cup (250 mL) finely
  chopped yellow onions
1 teaspoon (5 mL) curry
  powder
¼ teaspoon (1 mL) sugar
¼ teaspoon (1 mL) Chinese
  chili powder
¼ cup (60 mL) cream
2 tablespoons (30 mL)
  American-style barbecue
  sauce or satay sauce
1 small red pepper, seeded
  and cut into thin slices
½ cup (125 mL) brandy, if
  desired

1. Remove shells from
shrimp. Cut each shrimp
down the back using point of
small sharp knife. Remove
vein. Rinse shrimp and pat
dry with paper toweling.
Combine egg white, corn-
starch and salt in bowl. Mix
well. Mix in shrimp. Let
stand 1 hour.

2. Heat oil in wok over
medium-high heat until it
reaches 375°F (190°C). Add

shrimp, one at a time, to oil
(cook only half at a time).
Fry until golden, about 2
minutes. Drain on absor-
bent paper.

3. Remove all but 2 tablespoons (30 mL) of the oil
from wok. Stir-fry onions,
curry powder, sugar and
chili powder in the oil 2
minutes. Add shrimp. Stir-
fry 1 minute. Add cream and
barbecue sauce. Cook and
stir 1 minute. Mix in red pepper. Remove from heat.

4. Arrange shrimp on serving plate and spoon sauce

over shrimp. If desired, heat
brandy in small saucepan
just until warm and pour
into small metal bowl. Place
bowl on serving plate with
shrimp. Carefully ignite
brandy using long wooden
match. Hold shrimp over
flame for a few seconds.
Makes 2 to 4 servings

Seafood Combination

8 ounces (225 g) fresh or thawed frozen sea scallops

8 ounces (225 g) fresh or thawed frozen shrimp

8 ounces (225 g) fresh or thawed frozen fish fillets

8 green onions

3 stalks celery

1 can (8 ounces or 225 g) water chestnuts

1 can (8 ounces or 225 g) bamboo shoots

4 tablespoons (60 mL) vegetable oil

8 ounces (225 g) cleaned, ready-to-cook squid, if desired

½ cup (125 mL) water

2 teaspoons (10 mL) cornstarch

1 teaspoon (5 mL) instant chicken bouillon granules

1 tablespoon (15 mL) soy sauce

2 teaspoons (10 mL) dry sherry

1. Rinse scallops with water, drain and cut into quarters. Remove shells and back veins from shrimp. Remove skin, if any, from fillets. Cut fillets into 1½-inch (4 cm) square pieces.

2. Cut onions and celery into thin diagonal slices. Drain water chestnuts and cut into halves. Drain bamboo shoots and cut into thin slices.

3. Heat 2 tablespoons (30 mL) of the oil in wok over

high heat. Stir-fry onions, celery, water chestnuts and bamboo shoots in the oil until crisp-tender, 2 minutes. Remove from wok.

4. Heat remaining 2 tablespoons (30 mL) oil in wok. Add scallops, shrimp, fish pieces and squid. Stir-fry

until all fish is cooked and opaque, about 3 minutes.

5. Blend water, cornstarch, bouillon, soy sauce and sherry. Pour mixture over fish mixture in wok. Cook and stir until liquid boils. Return vegetables to wok. Cook and stir 2 minutes. Serve with Fried Noodles.
Makes 4 to 6 servings

Scallops with Vegetables

1 ounce (30 g) dried mushrooms

Boiling water

1 pound (450 g) fresh or thawed frozen sea scallops

2 medium yellow onions

3 stalks celery

8 ounces (225 g) fresh green beans

6 green onions

2 tablespoons (30 mL) vegetable oil

2 teaspoons (10 mL) grated pared fresh ginger root

1 clove garlic, crushed

4 teaspoons (20 mL) cornstarch

1 cup (250 mL) water

2½ tablespoons (37 mL) dry sherry

4 teaspoons (20 mL) soy sauce

2 teaspoons (10 mL) instant chicken bouillon granules

1 can (15 ounces or 425 g) baby corn, drained

1. Place mushrooms in bowl and cover with boiling water. Let stand 30 minutes. Drain. Squeeze out excess water. Cut into thin slices.

2. Rinse scallops and drain. Trim, if necessary, and cut into quarters.

3. Peel yellow onions, cut into wedges and separate layers. Cut celery into ½-inch (1.5 cm) diagonal slices. Wash and trim green beans. Cut beans into 1-inch (2.5 cm) diagonal slices. Cut green onions into thin diagonal slices.

4. Heat oil in wok over high heat. Add onions, celery, beans, ginger and garlic to oil. Stir-fry 3 minutes.

5. Measure cornstarch into small bowl. Blend in a few tablespoons of the water and mix until smooth. Stir in the remaining water, the sherry, soy sauce and bouillon. Add to vegetable mixture. Cook and stir until mixture boils.

6. Add scallops, mushrooms, green onions and corn. Cook and stir until scallops are tender, about 4 minutes.
Makes 4 to 6 servings

Crab-Stuffed Shrimp

SAUCE
- 2 tablespoons (30 mL) vegetable oil
- 1 small yellow onion, finely chopped
- 1 teaspoon (5 mL) curry powder
- 1½ tablespoons (22 mL) dry sherry
- 1 tablespoon (15 mL) satay sauce
- 1 teaspoon (5 mL) sugar
- 2 teaspoons (10 mL) soy sauce
- ¼ cup (60 mL) cream or milk

SHRIMP
- 2 cans (6½ ounces or 185 g each) crabmeat
- 2 egg whites
- 4 teaspoons (20 mL) cornstarch
- 1 tablespoon (15 mL) dry sherry
- 1 tablespoon (15 mL) soy sauce
- 8 green onions, finely chopped
- 2 stalks celery, finely chopped
- 1½ pounds (675 g) fresh uncooked large shrimp
- ½ cup (125 mL) all-purpose flour
- 3 eggs
- 3 tablespoons (45 mL) milk
- 2 to 3 cups (500 to 750 mL) soft bread crumbs (from 8 to 12 slices bread)
- 3 cups (750 mL) vegetable oil

For Sauce

1. Heat oil in small saucepan. Cook onion in the oil over medium heat until transparent, about 3 minutes. Add curry powder. Cook and stir 1 minute. Add sherry, satay sauce, sugar and soy sauce. Cook and stir 2 minutes. Blend in cream. Bring to boil. Boil 2 minutes. Keep warm.

For Shrimp

2. Drain and flake crabmeat. Blend egg whites, cornstarch, sherry and soy sauce in bowl. Add crabmeat, onions and celery. Mix well.

3. Remove shells from shrimp, leaving tail intact. Remove back veins from shrimp. Cut deep slit into but not through back of each shrimp. Flatten shrimp by pounding gently with mallet or rolling pin.

4. Spoon crabmeat mixture onto each shrimp and press into shrimp with back of spoon or small spatula.

5. Coat each shrimp lightly with flour. Beat eggs and milk with fork in shallow bowl until blended. Place each shrimp, stuffed side up, in egg mixture then spoon mixture over shrimp to cover completely. Coat each shrimp completely with bread crumbs, pressing crumbs lightly onto shrimp. Place shrimp in single layer on cookie sheets or plates. Refrigerate 30 minutes.

6. Heat oil in wok over medium-high heat until it reaches 375°F (190°C). Fry 4 or 5 shrimp at a time in the oil until golden, about 3 minutes. Drain on absorbent paper. Serve with warm sauce.

Makes 4 servings

Shrimp Toast

- 12 fresh uncooked large shrimp
- 1 egg
- 2½ tablespoons (37 mL) cornstarch
- ¼ teaspoon (1 mL) salt
- Pinch pepper
- 3 slices sandwich bread
- 1 hard-cooked egg yolk
- 1 slice cooked ham (about 1 ounce or 30 g)
- 1 green onion
- 2 cups (500 mL) vegetable oil

1. Remove shells from shrimp, leaving tails intact. Remove back veins from shrimp. Cut down back of shrimp with sharp knife. Gently press shrimp with fingers to flatten.

2. Beat 1 egg, cornstarch, salt and pepper with fork in small bowl until blended. Add shrimp to egg mixture and toss until shrimp are completely coated.

3. Remove crusts from bread. Cut each slice into quarters. Place one shrimp, cut side down, on each bread piece. Gently press shrimp

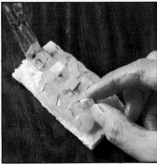

to adhere to bread. Brush or rub small amount of egg mixture over each shrimp.

4. Cut egg yolk and ham into ½-inch (1.5 cm) pieces. Finely chop onion. Place one piece each of egg yolk and ham and a scant ¼ teaspoon (1 mL) chopped onion on each shrimp.

5. Heat oil in wok over medium-high heat until it reaches 375°F (190°C). Fry 3 or 4 shrimp-bread pieces at a time in the hot oil until golden, 1 to 2 minutes on each side. Drain on absorbent paper.

Makes 1 dozen

Ginger Chili Fish

SAUCE

1 can (8 ounces or 225 g) tomato sauce

2 tablespoons (30 mL) dry sherry

1 tablespoon (15 mL) grated pared fresh ginger root

1 tablespoon (15 mL) Chinese chili sauce

1 tablespoon (15 mL) water

1 tablespoon (15 mL) soy sauce

2 teaspoons (10 mL) sugar

3 cloves garlic, crushed

FISH

1 pound (450 g) fresh or thawed frozen fish fillets

1 cup (250 mL) all-purpose flour

⅓ cup (80 mL) cornstarch

¾ cup (180 mL) water

1 egg white

½ teaspoon (2 mL) salt

3 cups (750 mL) vegetable oil

For Sauce

1. Combine all ingredients in medium saucepan. Cook over medium heat until sauce boils. Boil and stir 2 minutes. Remove from heat.

For Fish

2. Remove skin from fillets. (To do this, rub some salt on fingers and grasp skin at tail-end of fish. With a sharp knife held at an angle,

separate fish from skin using a sawing motion.) Cut fillets into 1-inch (2.5 cm) pieces.

3. Combine flour, cornstarch, water, egg white and salt. Beat with whisk until smooth.

4. Heat oil in wok over high heat until it reaches 375°F (190°C). Dip fish pieces, a few at a time, in batter, drain slightly, then place in the hot oil. Cook until fish is golden and completely cooked,

about 5 minutes. Drain on absorbent paper.

5. Remove oil from wok. Place fish and sauce in wok. Cook over medium heat, tossing lightly, until fish is hot throughout and completely coated with sauce, about 2 minutes.

Makes 4 servings

Crispy Fish with Lemon Sauce

LEMON SAUCE

1 cup (250 mL) water

1 piece lemon rind (about 1-inch or 2.5 cm square)

⅓ cup (80 mL) lemon juice

3 tablespoons (45 mL) packed brown sugar

1 piece fresh ginger root (about 1-inch or 2.5 cm square), pared and cut into thin slices

1 teaspoon (5 mL) instant chicken bouillon granules

1½ tablespoons (22 mL) cornstarch

2 tablespoons (30 mL) water

FISH

¾ cup (180 mL) all-purpose flour

2 whole fish (about 12 ounces or 340 g each), cleaned and scaled

6 tablespoons (90 mL) water

1½ teaspoons (7 mL) vegetable oil

3 cups (750 mL) vegetable oil

1 egg white

4 green onions, thinly sliced

For Sauce

1. Combine water, lemon rind and juice, sugar, ginger and bouillon in saucepan. Cook over medium-high heat until mixture boils. Reduce heat and simmer uncovered 5 minutes. Remove from heat. Strain sauce and return it to saucepan.

2. Blend cornstarch and the remaining 2 tablespoons (30 mL) water. Stir mixture into sauce. Cook and stir until sauce boils and thickens. Simmer 5 minutes, stirring frequently. Keep warm.

For Fish

3. Measure ¼ cup (60 mL) of the flour into a shallow dish. Coat fish on both sides lightly with the flour.

4. Combine remaining ½ cup (125 mL) flour, the water and 1½ teaspoons (7 mL) vegetable oil in large bowl. Beat with a whisk until smooth.

5. Heat 3 cups (750 mL) vegetable oil in wok over high heat until it reaches

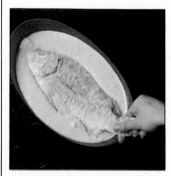

375°F (190°C). Reduce heat as needed to maintain temperature.

6. Beat egg white with electric mixer until stiff but not dry peaks form. Fold white

into batter. Dip fish in flour mixture, turning to coat completely. Drain off excess batter. Carefully place fish into oil (if wok is small, it may be necessary to cook fish separately). Cook until fish is golden and completely cooked, 8 to 10 minutes. Turn fish over once during cooking if necessary to cook evenly. Drain on absorbent paper.

7. Place fish on serving plate. Stir onions into Lemon Sauce and pour over fish.

Makes 2 servings

Crab Claws

Sweet and Sour Sauce (see Index for page number)

½ cup (125 mL) drained sliced Chinese Mixed Pickles (see Index for page number)

10 thick crab claws (about 1½ to 2 pounds or 675 to 900 g)

1½ pounds (675 g) fresh uncooked medium shrimp

6 green onions

2 stalks celery

2 teaspoons (10 mL) minced pared fresh ginger root

2 teaspoons (10 mL) soy sauce

2 teaspoons (10 mL) oyster sauce

1 cup (250 mL) cornstarch

½ cup (125 mL) all-purpose flour

½ teaspoon (2 mL) baking powder

½ teaspoon (2 mL) salt

⅔ cup (160 mL) water

4 cups (1 L) vegetable oil

1. Prepare Sweet and Sour Sauce. Stir Chinese Mixed Pickles into sauce. Keep sauce warm.

2. Carefully remove the shell from the meat end of each claw using kitchen shears, crab or nut cracker. If necessary, tap claw gently with a mallet or rolling pin to break shell (do not hit heavily or crabmeat will be damaged). Leave shell on one part of the pincher for holding the crabmeat.

3. Remove shells and back veins from shrimp. Chop shrimp, onions and celery very finely using a cleaver, sharp knife or food processor. Transfer chopped ingredients to a bowl. Add ginger, soy and oyster sauces. Mix well. Divide mixture into 10 equal portions (about ⅓ cup or 80 mL each). Flatten one portion out in palm of one hand. Place meat end of a crab claw on top of flattened shrimp mixture. Carefully press shrimp mixture all around crabmeat, leaving shell on pincher uncovered.

4. Measure ½ cup (125 mL) of the cornstarch into small bowl. Carefully coat each

shrimp-wrapped claw with the cornstarch.

5. Combine remaining ½ cup (125 mL) cornstarch, the flour, baking powder and salt. Using a whisk, gradually blend in water. Beat until smooth.

6. Heat oil in wok over medium-high heat until it reaches 375°F (190°C). Carefully dip each claw into batter, coating completely. Fry claws, a few at a time, in oil until golden and cooked through, 3 to 5 minutes. Drain on absorbent paper. Serve with Sweet and Sour Sauce.

Makes 5 servings

Shrimp Omelets

1 cup (250 mL) water
4 teaspoons (20 mL) cornstarch
1 teaspoon (5 mL) sugar
2 teaspoons (10 mL) soy sauce
2 teaspoons (10 mL) instant chicken bouillon granules
8 eggs
½ teaspoon (2 mL) salt
⅛ teaspoon (0.5 mL) pepper
8 fresh medium mushrooms
3 tablespoons (45 mL) vegetable oil
8 ounces (225 g) bean sprouts
8 ounces (225 g) fresh shrimp
4 green onions
1 stalk celery
2 green onions, thinly sliced

1. Combine water, cornstarch, sugar, soy sauce and bouillon in small saucepan. Cook over medium heat until mixture boils and thickens, about 5 minutes.

2. Combine eggs, salt and pepper in medium bowl. Beat until frothy.

3. Finely chop mushrooms. Heat 1 tablespoon (15 mL) of the oil in small skillet. Cook mushrooms in the oil 1 minute. Stir mushrooms into egg mixture.

4. Wash and drain sprouts. Remove shells and veins from shrimp. Finely chop shrimp, 4 of the onions and celery. Mix sprouts, shrimp, chopped onions and celery into egg mixture.

5. For *each* omelet, heat ½ tablespoon (7 mL) of the oil in large skillet or 7-inch (18 cm) omelet pan. Cook over medium heat until hot. Pour ½ cup (125 mL) egg mixture

into oil. Cook until light brown, 2 to 3 minutes on each side. Stack omelets on serving plates. Pour warm soy sauce mixture over omelets. Garnish with sliced green onions.

*Makes 4 servings
(2 omelets each)*

Butterfly Shrimp

1½ pounds (675 g) fresh large shrimp
3 egg yolks
1½ teaspoons (7 mL) cornstarch
½ teaspoon (2 mL) salt
⅛ teaspoon (0.5 mL) pepper
2 slices bacon
2 cups (500 mL) vegetable oil

1. Remove shells from shrimp, leaving tails intact. Cut each shrimp down the back using point of small sharp knife. Remove vein. Rinse shrimp and pat dry with paper toweling. Cut deep slit down back of each shrimp.

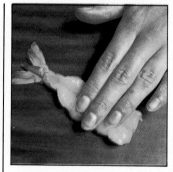

2. Flatten cut side slightly with fingers.

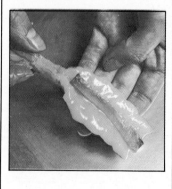

3. Beat egg yolks, cornstarch, salt and pepper with fork. Dip each shrimp into mixture. Cut bacon into 1½ x¼-inch (4x0.5 cm) strips. Place a bacon strip on cut side of each shrimp.

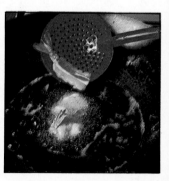

4. Heat oil in wok over medium-high heat until it reaches 400°F (200°C). Fry shrimp, a few at a time, in oil until golden, 2 to 3 minutes. Drain on absorbent paper.

*Makes 4 to 6 entree or
8 to 10 appetizer servings*

Crab in Ginger Sauce

2 ready-to-cook whole hard-shell crabs
8 green onions
1 small red pepper
1 piece (about 4x1-inch or 10x2.5 cm) fresh ginger root
¾ cup (180 mL) water
2½ tablespoons (37 mL) dry sherry
1 teaspoon (5 mL) sugar
1 teaspoon (5 mL) instant chicken bouillon granules
2 teaspoons (10 mL) soy sauce
2 teaspoons (10 mL) cornstarch
2 tablespoons (30 mL) vegetable oil
½ teaspoon (2 mL) sesame oil

1. Rinse crabs with water. Gently pull away round hard shell on top. With small sharp knife gently cut away the gray spongy tissue and discard. Rinse crabs with water.

2. Cut off claws and legs. Pound claws lightly with back of cleaver to break shell. Chop down center of crabs to cut body in half. Cut each half crosswise into 3 pieces.

3. Cut onions into 1-inch (2.5 cm) pieces. Remove seeds from pepper. Cut pepper into thin strips. Pare ginger root. Cut ginger into

thin slices, then cut the slices into very thin strips.

4. Combine ½ cup (125 mL) of the water, the sherry, sugar, bouillon and soy sauce. Combine remaining ¼ cup (60 mL) water and the cornstarch. Blend well.

5. Heat vegetable and sesame oils in wok over medium heat. Stir-fry ginger in the oils 1 minute. Add cut-up crabs. Stir-fry 1 minute.

6. Add sherry mixture and pepper to crab. Stir-fry over high heat until liquid boils. Reduce heat to low. Simmer covered 4 minutes. Uncover and stir in cornstarch mixture. Cook until sauce thickens. Add onions. Cook and stir 1 minute.
Makes 4 to 6 servings

Braised Shrimp with Vegetables

1 pound (450 g) fresh, uncooked large shrimp
8 ounces (225 g) fresh broccoli
2 cans (4 ounces or 115 g each) whole button mushrooms
1 can (8 ounces or 225 g) whole or sliced bamboo shoots
1 tablespoon (15 mL) vegetable oil
½ cup (125 mL) chicken stock or broth
1 teaspoon (5 mL) cornstarch
1 teaspoon (5 mL) oyster sauce
¼ teaspoon (1 mL) sugar
½ teaspoon (2 mL) grated, pared fresh ginger root
⅛ teaspoon (0.5 mL) pepper

1. Remove shells and back veins from shrimp.

2. Cut broccoli into pieces. Drain mushrooms. Cut whole bamboo shoots into thin slices.

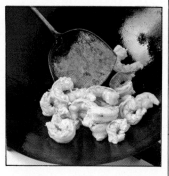

3. Heat oil in wok over high heat. Stir-fry shrimp in oil until tender, about 3 minutes.

4. Add broccoli to shrimp. Stir-fry 1 minute. Add mushrooms and bamboo shoots. Stir-fry 1 minute longer.

5. Combine remaining ingredients. Pour mixture over shrimp-vegetable mixture. Cook and stir until liquid boils. Cook and stir 1 minute longer.
Makes 4 servings

Chinese Vegetables

1 pound (450 g) fresh
    broccoli
8 ounces (225 g) fresh
    spinach
8 ounces (225 g) fresh pea
    pods or 1 package (6
    ounces or 170 g) frozen
    pea pods, thawed
4 stalks celery
2 medium yellow onions
8 green onions
¾ cup (180 mL) water
1 tablespoon (15 mL)
    instant chicken bouillon
    granules
2 tablespoons (30 mL)
    vegetable oil
1 tablespoon (15 mL)
    minced pared fresh
    ginger root

Note: Sliced carrots, zucchini, green beans, or green peppers may be used in addition to or in place of the listed vegetables.

2. Heat oil in wok over high heat. Add broccoli stalks, onion wedges and ginger. Stir-fry 1 minute.

3. Add all remaining vegetables. Toss lightly.

1. Clean vegetables. Cut broccoli tops into flowerettes. Cut broccoli stalks into thin strips 2 inches (5 cm) long and ¼ inch (0.5 cm) wide. Chop spinach coarsely. Remove ends and strings from pea pods. Cut celery into ½-inch (1.5 cm) diagonal slices. Peel yellow onions, cut into wedges and separate layers. Cut green onions into thin diagonal slices. Combine water and bouillon.

4. Add water mixture. Toss until vegetables are completely coated. Cook until liquid boils. Cover wok and cook until vegetables are crisp-tender, 2 to 3 minutes.
Makes 4 to 6 servings

Bean Curd with Oyster Sauce

8 ounces (225 g) bean curd
4 ounces (225 g) fresh
　mushrooms
6 green onions
3 stalks celery
1 red or green pepper
2 tablespoons (30 mL)
　vegetable oil
½ cup (125 mL) water
1 tablespoon (15 mL)
　cornstarch
2 tablespoons (30 mL)
　oyster sauce
4 teaspoons (20 mL) dry
　sherry
4 teaspoons (20 mL) soy
　sauce

1. Cut bean curd into ½-inch (1.5 cm) cubes. Clean mushrooms and cut into slices. Cut onions into 1-inch (2.5 cm) pieces. Cut celery into ½-inch (1.5 cm) diagonal slices. Remove seeds from pepper and cut pepper into ½-inch (1.5 cm) chunks.

2. Heat 1 tablespoon (15 mL) of the oil in wok over high heat. Cook bean curd in the oil, stirring gently, until light brown, 3 minutes. Remove from pan.

3. Heat remaining 1 tablespoon (15 mL) oil in wok over high heat. Add mushrooms, onions, celery and pepper. Stir-fry 1 minute.

4. Return bean curd to wok. Toss lightly to combine. Blend water, cornstarch, oyster sauce, sherry and soy

sauce. Pour over mixture in wok. Cook and stir until liquid boils. Cook and stir 1 minute longer.

Makes 4 servings

Chinese Mixed Pickles

PICKLING LIQUID
3 cups (750 mL) sugar
3 cups (750 mL) white
　vinegar
1½ cups (375 mL) water
1½ teaspoons (7 mL) salt

PICKLES
3 large carrots
1 large Chinese white
　radish (about 1 pound or
　450 g)
1 large cucumber
4 stalks celery
8 green onions
4 ounces (115 g) fresh
　ginger root
1 large red pepper
1 large green pepper

For Pickling Liquid
1. Combine all ingredients in 3 quart (3 L) saucepan. Cook and stir over medium heat until liquid boils. Remove from heat. Cool.

For Pickles
2. Wash all vegetables. Pare carrots and radish. Cut cucumber lengthwise into quarters and remove seeds. Cut carrots, radish and cucumber into "match stick" thin strips about 2 inches (5 cm) long. Cut celery into ½-inch (1.5 cm) diagonal slices. Cut onions into

¼-inch (0.5 cm) diagonal slices. Pare ginger root and cut into thin slices. Remove seeds from peppers and cut peppers into ½-inch (1.5 cm) cubes.

3. Fill a 5-quart (5 L) Dutch oven half full of water. Cover and cook over high heat until water boils. Uncover and add all vegetables. Remove from heat immediately. Let vegetables stand uncovered 2 minutes.

4. Drain vegetables in large colander. Spread vegetables out on clean towels and allow to dry 2 or 3 hours.

5. Pack vegetables firmly into clean jars with lids. Pour Pickling Liquid into jars until vegetables are completely covered. Cover jars tightly. Store in refrigerator at least 1 week before using.

*Makes 1½ to 2 quarts
(1.5 to 2 L)*

RICE AND NOODLES

Fried Rice

3 cups (750 mL) water
1½ teaspoons (7 mL) salt
1½ cups (375 mL)
    uncooked long grain rice
4 slices bacon, chopped
3 eggs
⅛ teaspoon (0.5 mL)
    pepper
3 tablespoons (45 mL)
    vegetable oil
2 teaspoons (10 mL) grated
    fresh ginger root
8 ounces (225 g) cooked
    pork, cut into thin strips
8 ounces (225 g) cooked,
    cleaned shrimp, coarsely
    chopped
8 green onions, finely
    chopped
1 to 2 tablespoons (15 to 30
    mL) soy sauce

1. Combine water and salt in 3-quart (3 L) saucepan. Cover and cook over high heat until boiling. Stir in rice. Cover, reduce heat and simmer until rice is tender, 15 to 20 minutes. (Or cook rice according to package directions.) Drain rice.

2. Cook bacon in wok over medium heat, stirring frequently, until crisp. Drain bacon. Remove all but 1 tablespoon (15 mL) of the drippings from wok.

3. Beat eggs and pepper with fork. Pour ⅓ of the egg mixture into wok. Tilt wok slightly so egg mixture covers bottom. Cook over medium heat until eggs are set, 1 to 2 minutes. Remove eggs from wok, roll up and

cut into thin strips. Pour ½ tablespoon (7 mL) of the oil into wok. Add ½ of the remaining egg mixture, tilt wok and cook until eggs are set. Remove eggs, roll up and cut thinly. Repeat procedure with ½ tablespoon (7 mL) of the remaining oil and remaining eggs. Remove eggs from wok and cut thinly.

4. Add remaining 2 tablespoons (30 mL) oil and the ginger to wok. Stir-fry over medium-high heat 1 minute. Stir in rice. Cook and stir 5 minutes. Stir in bacon, pork, shrimp, onions and soy sauce. Cook and stir until hot throughout.
Makes 6 to 8 servings

Vermicelli

8 ounces (225 g) Chinese rice vermicelli or bean threads

3 cups (750 mL) vegetable oil

1. Cut bundle of vermicelli in half. Gently pull each half apart into small bunches.

2. Heat oil in wok over medium-high heat until 375°F (190°C). Using long handled tongs or spoon, place a bunch of vermicelli in the hot oil (cook only one small bunch at a time.)

3. Cook until vermicelli rises to the top, 3 to 5 seconds. Immediately remove vermicelli from oil with tongs or slotted spoon. Drain on absorbent paper. Repeat to cook remaining bunches.

4. Serve vermicelli as desired separately or with other foods.

Makes about 4 servings

Noodle Baskets

8 ounces (225 g) Chinese-style thin egg noodles

Water

Salt

3 cups (750 mL) vegetable oil

Note: Noodle Baskets can be cooked, wrapped securely in plastic and stored in refrigerator up to three days or in freezer up to three weeks. To reheat, remove from plastic, spread on cookie sheet and bake in preheated 325°F (160°C) oven until hot throughout, 8 to 10 minutes.

1. Cook noodles in boiling salted water according to package directions just until tender. Drain noodles in colander.

2. Arrange several layers of paper toweling over jelly roll pan or cookie sheet. Spread noodles evenly over paper toweling. Let dry at least 8 hours or overnight.

3. Brush inside of medium strainer (about 5 inches or 13 cm in diameter) with a little of the oil. Spread an even layer of noodles about ½-inch (1.5 cm) thick in strainer. Brush the outside rounded side of another medium strainer with oil. Place second strainer, rounded side down, over noodles in first strainer. Press lightly.

4. Heat oil in wok over medium-high heat until it reaches 375°F (190°C). Carefully lower the two strainers, holding handles together, into the oil. Fry until noodles are golden, 2 to 3 minutes. Remove from oil and place on absorbent paper. Carefully remove top and bottom strainers, running knife blade around edge of noodles if necessary to loosen. Drain baskets on paper. Repeat to cook remaining noodles.

Makes 6 to 8 baskets

Fried Noodles

8 ounces (225 g)
   Chinese-style thin egg
   noodles
Water
Salt
3 cups (750 mL) vegetable
   oil

1. Cook noodles in boiling salted water according to package directions just until tender. Drain noodles in colander.

2. Arrange several layers of paper toweling over jelly roll pan or cookie sheet. Spread noodles evenly over paper toweling. Let dry 2 to 3 hours.

3. Heat oil in wok over medium-high heat until it reaches 375°F (190°C).

4. Using long-handled tongs or slotted spoon, cook small amount of noodles at a time in oil until golden, about 30 seconds.

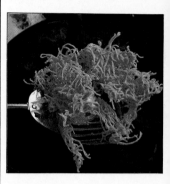

5. Remove noodles from oil. Drain on absorbent paper. Repeat to cook remaining noodles.
Makes about 4 servings

Steamed Rice

1 cup (250 mL) long-grain
   rice
2 cups (500 mL) water
1 teaspoon (5 mL) salt
1 tablespoon (15 mL)
   vegetable oil

1. Place rice in strainer and rinse well under cold running water to remove excess starch.

2. Combine rice, water, salt and oil in 3-quart (3 L) saucepan.

3. Cook over medium-high heat until water boils. Reduce heat to low. Cover pan and simmer until rice is tender, 15 to 20 minutes.

4. Remove pan from heat. Let stand 5 minutes. Uncover pan and fluff rice lightly with fork. Serve as desired.
Makes 3 cups (750 mL)

DESSERTS

Watermelon in Ginger Wine

Chinese cuisine does not offer a wide range of desserts. We have included a few traditional recipes in this section, and have added some light and lovely desserts which make a superb ending to a Chinese meal.

½ watermelon
1 cup (250 mL) water
½ cup (125 mL) ginger wine
2 tablespoons (30 mL) sugar
1 ounce (30 g) preserved candied ginger

1. Shape watermelon into balls using a round melon baller, removing seeds from

melon as necessary. When all melon on top surface has been shaped, cut off top using a long sharp knife. Scoop out the exposed surface of melon.

2. Combine melon balls in large bowl.

3. Combine water, wine and sugar in small saucepan. Cook over medium heat, stirring until sugar dissolves and mixture is hot. Remove from heat.

4. Cut ginger into thin slivers. Stir ginger into wine mixture. Pour over melon balls. Refrigerate several hours or overnight, stirring occasionally.

5. Spoon watermelon and wine mixture into serving bowls.
Makes 4 to 6 servings

Almond Crème

¾ cup (180 mL) cold water
1 envelope unflavored
 gelatin
½ cup (125 mL) sugar
¾ cup (180 mL) boiling
 water
1¼ cups (310 mL)
 evaporated milk
½ teaspoon (2 mL) vanilla
½ teaspoon (2 mL) almond
 extract
2 kiwi fruits, if desired
4 fresh ripe strawberries,
 if desired

1. Measure cold water into small bowl. Sprinkle gelatin over cold water. Let stand 1 minute.

2. Add sugar to gelatin mixture. Stir until gelatin dissolves. Pour boiling water into medium bowl. Stir in gelatin mixture.

3. Combine milk, vanilla and almond extract. Stir milk mixture into gelatin mixture.

4. Divide mixture between four serving dishes. Refrigerate until set, about 3 hours.

5. Pare and slice kiwis. Arrange kiwi slices and strawberries over each dessert.

Makes 4 servings

Banana Fritters

1½ cups (375 mL) all-
 purpose flour
1 teaspoon (5 mL) baking
 powder
¼ teaspoon (1 mL) baking
 soda
¼ teaspoon (1 mL) salt
¾ cup (180 mL) water
4 firm bananas
3 cups (750 mL) vegetable
 oil
Vanilla ice cream, if desired

1. Combine 1 cup (250 mL) of the flour, the baking powder, soda and salt in large bowl.

2. Gradually blend in water beating with a whisk until smooth.

3. Peel bananas. Cut each banana crosswise into 3 pieces, making a total of 12 pieces. Coat bananas lightly with remaining ½ cup (125 mL) flour.

4. Heat oil in wok over medium-high heat until it reaches 375°F (190°C). Dip banana pieces in flour-water mixture, coating completely. Cook 4 to 6 banana pieces at a time in the oil until golden, 3 to 5 minutes. Drain on absorbent paper. Serve with ice cream.

Makes about 4 servings

Lychees and Mandarin Ice

2 cups (500 mL) water
½ cup (125 mL) sugar
2 cans (11 ounces or 310 g each) mandarin orange segments
¼ cup (60 mL) lemon juice
2 tablespoons (30 mL) orange-flavored liqueur
1 can (20 ounces or 565 g) peeled whole lychees

1. Measure water and sugar into medium saucepan. Cook over low heat, stirring constantly, until mixture boils. Boil and stir 3 minutes. Remove from heat. Cool.

2. Place one can of mandarin oranges with syrup into 5-cup (1250 mL) blender container. Blend until smooth, about 1 minute. Strain mixture.

3. Stir blended oranges, lemon juice and liqueur into cooled sugar mixture. Pour into 1½-quart (1.5 L) rectangular baking pan or dish. Freeze until firm, at least 3 hours.

4. Refrigerate lychees and remaining mandarin oranges until cold.

5. To serve, drain lychees, reserving syrup, and oranges. Spoon fruit and lychee syrup into serving dishes.

6. Remove frozen fruit mixture from freezer. Flake lightly with fork and spoon over fruit in each dish.

Makes about 4 servings

Melon with Champagne

1 small honeydew melon
½ cup (125 mL) water
½ cup (125 mL) sugar
¼ cup (60 mL) ginger wine
Champagne
1 pound (450 g) medium seedless green grapes
1 egg white
1 cup (250 mL) super-fine granulated sugar

1. Cut melon in half and remove the seeds. Shape melon into balls using small melon baller. Place melon balls in bowl, cover with plastic wrap and refrigerate until cold.

2. Combine water, sugar and wine in small saucepan. Cook over medium heat, stirring until sugar dissolves. Cook until mixture boils. Let boil 3 minutes. Remove pan from heat and refrigerate until cold. Refrigerate champagne until cold.

3. Cut grapes into 6 small bunches, leaving a large enough stem section on each to hook over the rim of a glass.

4. Beat egg white in small bowl with fork until frothy. Brush egg white completely over grapes.

5. Immediately place grapes in sugar, turning to coat completely. Place grapes on large plate and let stand 2 hours.

6. Divide melon balls between 6 large wine glasses. Spoon about 2 tablespoons (30 mL) ginger-syrup mixture over melon in each glass. Fill glass with champagne. Hang a bunch of grapes over outside edge of each glass.

Makes 6 servings

Toffee Apples

2 medium green cooking
   apples
1 cup (250 mL) all-purpose
   flour
2 cups (500 mL) water
3 teaspoons (15 mL) sesame
   oil
3 cups (750 mL) vegetable
   oil
2 cups (500 mL) sugar
2 tablespoons (30 mL)
   sesame seeds
Cold water
Ice cubes

1. Pare apples, cut into quarters and remove cores. Cut each quarter in half crosswise, making 16 pieces total.

2. Measure flour into bowl. Gradually blend in 1 cup (250 mL) of the water using a whisk. Add 2 teaspoons (10 mL) of the sesame oil. Beat until smooth.

3. Brush remaining 1 teaspoon (5 mL) sesame oil over a serving plate. Set aside.

4. Place apple pieces in batter, turning to coat completely.

5. Heat 3 cups (750 mL) vegetable oil in wok over medium-high heat until it reaches 375°F (190°C). Using a slotted spoon, lift apple pieces from batter and place in oil. Cook half of the pieces at a time until light brown, about 2 minutes. Drain on absorbent paper.

6. Pour oil out of wok but do not clean wok. Measure

remaining 1 cup (250 mL) water and the sugar into wok. Cook, stirring constantly, until mixture reaches about 235°F (113°C) on a candy thermometer, 10 to 13 minutes.

7. Remove from heat immediately. Mix in apples and sesame seeds. Transfer to the oiled serving plate. Place cold water and ice cubes in bowl. Dunk apples in the ice water before eating.
Makes about 4 servings

Strawberry Sorbet

1 pint (500 mL) fresh ripe
   strawberries
1 cup (250 mL) water
¾ cup (180 mL) super-fine
   granulated sugar
2½ tablespoons (37 mL)
   lemon juice
2½ tablespoons (37 mL)
   orange flavored liqueur
2 egg whites
¼ teaspoon (1 mL) cream
   of tartar
Watermelon, cut into
   1-inch (2.5 cm) pieces,
   if desired

1. Wash and hull strawberries. Place berries, water, ½ cup (125 mL) of the sugar, the lemon juice and liqueur in 5-cup (1250 mL) blender container. Blend until smooth, about 2 minutes.

2. Pour strawberry mixture through a strainer into an 11 x 7-inch (28 x 18 cm) baking pan. Freeze until firm, 3 to 4 hours.

3. Beat egg whites and cream of tartar in bowl until foamy. Add remaining ¼ cup (60 mL) sugar, 1 table-

spoon (15 mL) at a time, beating constantly until sugar is dissolved and whites stand in soft peaks.

4. Remove strawberry mixture from freezer. Flake with a fork. Spoon egg whites over strawberry mixture.

Gently but thoroughly fold whites into strawberry mixture. Freeze until firm, at least 2 hours.

5. Spoon into serving dishes over watermelon.
Makes 6 servings

Chocolate Ginger Lychees

1 can (20 ounces or 565 g)
  whole peeled lychees
2 ounces (60 g) preserved
  candied ginger
6 ounces (170 g) semi-sweet
  baking chocolate
  (6 squares)
1 tablespoon (15 mL)
  vegetable shortening

1. Drain lychees. Spread lychees round side up between several layers of paper toweling. Let stand until dry, about 1 hour.

2. Cut ginger into slivers or tiny pieces. Carefully stuff ginger inside cavities of lychees.

3. Combine chocolate and shortening in small saucepan or in top of double boiler over boiling water. Cook over low heat, stirring constantly, just until chocolate melts. Remove from heat. Cool slightly.

4. Dip each lychee in chocolate to coat completely. Carefully lift lychee out of chocolate and place round side up on greased parchment or waxed paper. Drizzle remaining chocolate over lychees. Refrigerate until cold.

Makes about 2 dozen

Custard Tarts

3 cups (750 mL) all-purpose
  flour
1 teaspoon (5 mL) salt
1 cup (250 mL) vegetable
  shortening or lard
4 to 6 tablespoons (60 to 90
  mL) hot tap water
3 eggs
⅓ cup (80 mL) sugar
1½ cups (375 mL) milk

4. Beat eggs with whisk. Stir in sugar and remaining ½ teaspoon (2 mL) salt. Gradually blend in milk.

1. Combine flour and ½ teaspoon (2 mL) of the salt in mixing bowl. Cut in shortening until mixture resembles bread crumbs. Mix in enough water to form a dough that sticks together. Shape dough into ball. Cut in half.

2. Roll out each half on lightly floured surface until ⅛-inch (0.5 cm) thick. Cut 12 circles from each half using fluted cookie cutter 3 inches (8 cm) in diameter.

3. Fit pastry circles into greased muffin cups, pressing sides so they reach rims.

Spoon about 2 tablespoons (30 mL) egg mixture into each pastry.

5. Bake in preheated 350°F (180°C) oven until knife inserted in center of custards comes out clean, 25 to 30 minutes. Remove tarts from pans. Cool on wire racks.

Makes 2 dozen

Sesame Peanut Candy

2 cups (500 mL) sugar
⅓ cup (80 mL) white
  vinegar
4 teaspoons (20 mL) water
½ cup (125 mL) sesame
  seeds, toasted*
1½ cups (375 mL) roasted
  unsalted skinless peanuts
  (about 8 ounces or
  225 g)

Note: To toast sesame seeds, sprinkle evenly into 11x7x1½-inch (28x18x4 cm) baking pan. Bake in preheated 350°F (180°C) oven until golden, about 5 minutes. Cool.

1. Combine sugar, vinegar and water in medium saucepan. Cook over low heat, stirring just until sugar dissolves. Cook without

stirring until mixture boils. Boil mixture without stirring until it is golden and reaches 295° to 300°F (146° to 149°C) or hard-crack stage on a candy thermometer, about 10 minutes.

2. While sugar mixture is boiling, grease an 11x7x1½-inch (28x18x4 cm) baking pan. Sprinkle half of the sesame seeds and all of the peanuts evenly into pan.

3. Pour sugar mixture over nuts in pan. Smooth surface with the back of a greased wooden spoon. Sprinkle with remaining sesame seeds. Cool slightly. While candy is still warm, cut it into 2x1-inch (5x2.5 cm) pieces. Cool completely. Remove from pan.
Makes 2½ to 3 dozen pieces

China Tea

For over a thousand years tea has been the drink of China. The Chinese drink it morning, noon and night; before, during and after meals. They never interfere with tea's natural flavor by adding sugar, lemon, cream or milk.

VARIETIES OF CHINESE TEA

There are many varieties of Chinese tea that differ greatly in character, flavor and aroma. Since the leaves for all Chinese teas come from the same plant (a member of the camellia family), the differences are a result of the processing techniques.

Green Tea: an unfermented tea that produces a light golden brew. Its leaves retain their natural green color and its taste is delicate. It's suitable for drinking day and night with most foods.

Black Tea: a fermented tea that produces a full bodied brew. Its leaves change color during fermentation from green to red to black. It's a good choice for accompanying full-flavored, spicy dishes and deep fried foods. Among the black teas, the most popular include Keemun, and Lapsang Souchong.

Oolong Tea: a semi-fermented tea that yields an amber brew. It combines the more pungent aroma of the black teas and the delicate fragrance of the green teas. The fermentation process is stopped midway, producing leaves that are brownish-green. Oolong tea is a good choice with distinctively flavored foods such as shrimp, fish, broccoli and cauliflower.

Scented Tea: a blend of tea leaves and fresh or dried flowers. Scented teas can be made from green, black or oolong varieties. They are good with many stir-fried dishes and are especially nice between meals. The most popular scented teas are jasmine, lychee and chrysanthemum.

BREWING CHINA TEA

There is no exact recipe for making Chinese teas. The amount required to brew a cup varies with the variety and nature of each tea. Unlike many other teas, the color of Chinese tea is not a good indicator of its strength of flavor. (It usually is stronger than its color suggests.) A general guideline is to use ½ to 1 teaspoon (2 to 5 mL) of tea for each 1 cup (250 mL) of water. Green teas are more potent than other varieties and should be used in smaller amounts.

Tea is generally made in a teapot—a china one (as opposed to metal) that must be clean. To brew the tea, scald the inside of the pot with boiling water (only freshly drawn water should be used), then discard the water. Add tea leaves. Pour in more boiling water. Cover the pot. Let it steep 3 to 5 minutes. Time the tea. Do not attempt to judge doneness by its color. If brewing tea in a cup, follow the same procedure, placing the leaves in the bottom of the cup rather than in a metal tea holder.

Most Chinese teas can be infused (brewed) more than once. In fact, many believe that the flavor of the second infusion is superior to the first. The second brewing is done exactly like the first without adding additional tea leaves.